SCHOLASTIC

BOOK OF WORLD RECORDS 2004

By Jenifer Corr Morse

A GEORGIAN BAY BOOK

SCHOLASTIC REFERENCE

To Bill and Rose Corr—the world's greatest parents.
–Jenifer Corr Morse

CREATED AND PRODUCED BY GEORGIAN BAY ASSOCIATES, LLC

Georgian Bay Staff
Bruce S. Glassman, Executive Editor
Jenifer Corr Morse, Photo Editor
Calico Harington, Design

Scholastic Reference Staff
Kenneth R. Wright, Editorial Director
Mary Varilla Jones, Editor
Elysa Jacobs, Assistant Editor
Nancy Sabato, Art Director
Dwayne Howard, Photo Researcher

In most cases, the graphs in this book represent the top five record holders in each category.
However, in some graphs, we have chosen to list well-known or common people, places,
animals, or things that will help you better understand how extraordinary the record holder
is. These may not be the top five in the category. Additionally, some graphs have fewer than
five entries because so few people or objects reflect the necessary criteria.

ISBN 0-439-54250-2

10 9 8 7 6 5 4 3 2 1   03 04 05 06 07
Printed in the U.S.A.   23
First printing, October 2003

Contents

Nature Records · 130

U.S. Records · 205

Human-Made Records · 256

Money and Business Records · 278

Popular Culture Records

Music • Television • Movies • Theater • Art

World's Top-Earning Male Singer

Paul McCartney

Former Beatle Paul McCartney earned a breathtaking $75 million in 2002. His total net worth is actually $1.2 billion, making him one of the thirty richest people in Britain. McCartney's very successful year is due in part to his wildly popular *Back in the USA* tour to promote his record, *Driving Rain*. It was McCartney's first tour in ten years and fans were thrilled to have him back. The 78,000 tickets to his first 6 shows sold out in less than 90 minutes. McCartney also performed at the Super Bowl, the Oscars®, and several fundraisers that year.

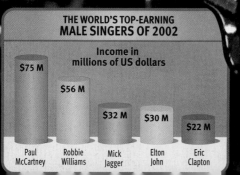

THE WORLD'S TOP-EARNING MALE SINGERS OF 2002

Income in millions of US dollars

Paul McCartney	Robbie Williams	Mick Jagger	Elton John	Eric Clapton
$75 M	$56 M	$32 M	$30 M	$22 M

World's Top-Earning Female Singer

Mariah Carey

Superstar Mariah Carey earned a whopping $58 million in 2002. In December of that year, Carey's *Charmbracelet* debuted at number three on the charts. Carey has been a singing sensation since her debut in 1990, setting many impressive records. Her songs have spent more weeks at number one on the Billboard charts than any other artist in history. More than 150 million of her albums and singles have been sold. Some of her best-selling albums include *Mariah Carey*, *Emotions*, and *Daydream*.

THE WORLD'S TOP-EARNING FEMALE SINGERS OF 2002

Income in millions of US dollars

Mariah Carey	Madonna	Britney Spears	Celine Dion	Jennifer Lopez
$58.0 M	$43.0 M	$39.2 M	$38.1 M	$37.0 M

Best-Selling
Single of All Time

Candle in the Wind 1997

**BEST-SELLING
SINGLES OF ALL TIME**

Sales in millions

- 37 M — "Candle in the Wind (1997)," Elton John
- 30 M — "White Christmas," Bing Crosby
- 25 M — "Rock Around the Clock," Bill Haley and the Comets
- 12 M — "I Want to Hold Your Hand," The Beatles
- 10 M — "Hey Jude," The Beatles

Elton John's single "Candle in the Wind 1997" sold a record-shattering 37 million copies since its release that year. John had first released the song in 1973 to honor the memory of Marilyn Monroe. When John's close friend Princess Diana was killed in a tragic car crash in 1997, John rewrote the song as a tribute to her and performed it at her funeral. John felt that this song was also especially appropriate for the princess because both women were constantly hounded by the press. John also earned a Grammy Award® for "Candle in the Wind 1997" for Best Male Pop Vocal Performance later that year.

World's Best-Selling Album

Thriller

To date, Michael Jackson's smash hit *Thriller* has sold approximately 46 million copies. It was first released on March 16, 1982, and quickly became one of the most popular albums of all time—both nationally and internationally. *Thriller* was released on the Epic record label and was produced by mastermind Quincy Jones. The album featured many pop singles, including "Beat It," "Billie Jean," and "Wanna Be Startin' Somethin." Thriller received eight Grammy® Awards and contained six top-ten singles.

THE WORLD'S BEST-SELLING ALBUMS

Albums sold in millions of copies

Thriller, Michael Jackson	46.0 M
The Bodyguard Soundtrack	36.0 M
Bat Out of Hell, Meatloaf	35.5 M
Dark Side of the Moon, Pink Floyd	28.2 M
Saturday Night Fever Soundtrack	27.0 M

World's Best-Selling
Recording Group

The Beatles

Since their first official recording session in September 1962, the Beatles have sold more than 164 million copies of their music. In the two years that followed, they had 26 top-40 singles. The "Fab Four," as they were called, were John Lennon, Paul McCartney, George Harrison, and Ringo Starr. Together they recorded many albums that are now considered rock masterpieces, such as *Rubber Soul*, *Sgt. Pepper's Lonely Hearts Club Band*, and *The White Album*. The group broke up in 1969. In 2001, however, their newly released greatest hits album—*The Beatles 1*—reached the top of the charts. In January 2003, some 500 never-before-heard tapes of the Beatles' recording sessions were discovered to the delight of fans around the world.

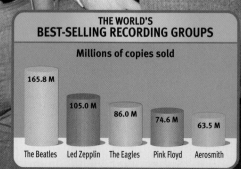

**THE WORLD'S
BEST-SELLING RECORDING GROUPS**

Millions of copies sold

The Beatles	Led Zepplin	The Eagles	Pink Floyd	Aerosmith
165.8 M	105.0 M	86.0 M	74.6 M	63.5 M

World's
Top-Earning Band

U2

U2—a four-man band from Ireland—earned $69 million in 2002. The group won several Grammy Awards® that year, including Record of the Year for "Walk On" and Best Rock Album for *All That You Can't Leave Behind*. Composed of lead singer Bono, guitarist The Edge, bassist Adam Clayton, and drummer Larry Mullin, U2 has been making music since 1978. After reaching the top of the UK charts, U2 quickly became a hit in the United States as well. Some of their most well-known albums include *The Joshua Tree* (1996), *Rattle and Hum* (1988), and *The Best of 1990–2000* (2000).

THE WORLD'S TOP-EARNING BANDS OF 2002

Earnings in millions of US dollars

U2	Dave Matthews Band	*NSYNC	Backstreet Boys	Aerosmith
$69.0 M	$50.0 M	$42.3 M	$36.8 M	$25.0 M

World's Best-Selling Male
Recording Artist

Garth Brooks

Country superstar Garth Brooks has sold 105 million copies of his recordings since his career took off in 1989. His first album, titled *Garth Brooks*, reached the fourth slot on the country charts. Brooks's third album—Grammy-winning *Ropin' the Wind*—became the first album in history to debut at number one on both the pop and country charts. Some of Brooks' other best-selling albums include *Sevens* (1997) and *Garth Brooks In . . . The Life of Chris Gaines* (1999). In November 2001, *Scarecrow* became Brooks's seventh album to debut at number one on the pop charts—a music industry first.

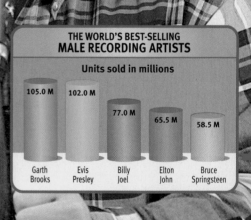

THE WORLD'S BEST-SELLING
MALE RECORDING ARTISTS

Units sold in millions

Garth Brooks	Evis Presley	Billy Joel	Elton John	Bruce Springsteen
105.0 M	102.0 M	77.0 M	65.5 M	58.5 M

World's Best-Selling Female Recording Artist

Barbra Streisand

During her 39 years as a singer, Barbra Streisand has sold over 68 million copies of her work. She has recorded more than 50 albums and has more gold albums than any other entertainer in history. Streisand has 47 gold albums, 28 platinum albums, 13 multiplatinum albums, 8 gold singles, 5 platinum singles, and 5 gold videos. Some of her recordings include *People*, *Color Me Barbra*, *Emotion*, and *Higher Ground*. Some of her best-known film work includes roles in *Funny Girl*, *The Way We Were*, *Yentl*, and *The Prince of Tides*. Streisand has won 10 Grammys®, 2 Academy Awards®, 6 Emmy Awards®, and 11 Golden Globes.

THE WORLD'S BEST-SELLING FEMALE RECORDING ARTISTS

Units sold, in millions

Barbra Streisand	Madonna	Mariah Carey	Whitney Houston	Celine Dion
68.5 M	60.0 M	53.5 M	53.0 M	42.5 M

Singer with the Most
Country Music Awards

Vince Gill

Country superstar Vince Gill has racked up 18 Country Music Awards. Since his debut album *Turn Me Loose* in 1984, Gill has been a fan favorite. He won his first Country Music Award in 1990 for Single of the Year with "When I Call Your Name." Since then, he has won Male Vocalist of the Year five times, Song of the Year four times, Vocal Event of the Year four times, Entertainer of the Year twice, and Album of the Year twice. Several of Gill's albums have gone gold and platinum, and he was asked to join the Grand Ole Opry in 1992.

SINGERS WITH THE MOST
COUNTRY MUSIC AWARDS

Number of awards

18	13	12	11	10
Vince Gill	Alan Jackson	Brooks & Dunn	Garth Brooks	Dixie Chicks

Most Popular Television Show

Friends

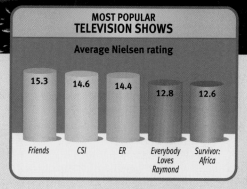

In 2002, NBC's hit comedy *Friends* was the most watched television show, with an average of 24.5 million viewers each week. The same year, Jennifer Aniston also picked up an Emmy Award for Best Actress in a Comedy Series. The series focuses on the lives of six close friends who live in New York City. The characters—Rachel, Monica, Phoebe, Ross, Joey, and Chandler— are played by Jennifer Aniston, Courteney Cox Arquette, Lisa Kudrow, David Schwimmer, Matt LeBlanc, and Matthew Perry. Even the show's production statistics are impressive. Some 36,000 feet (10,980 m) of film is used to tape just one episode. It takes 366,000 watts of electricity to light the set for one filming. That's the equivalent of powering 12 large homes!

MOST POPULAR TELEVISION SHOWS

Average Nielsen rating

Friends	CSI	ER	Everybody Loves Raymond	Survivor: Africa
15.3	14.6	14.4	12.8	12.6

Highest-Paid
TV Actresses

Jennifer Aniston, Courteney Cox Arquette, and Lisa Kudrow of the hit TV sitcom *Friends* each earn $1 million per episode. Millions of fans have tuned in to see Rachel Green, Monica Geller, and Phoebe Buffay figure out relationships, work, and everyday life in New York City. Since the series began, the show has received 44 Emmy® nominations, including Kudrow's Best Supporting Actress win in 1998. Aniston recently won a Golden Globe for Best Actress in 2002. The show has also been nominated for several People's Choice Awards and won a Screen Actor's Guild Award in 1996.

Jennifer Aniston, Courteney Cox Arquette, Lisa Kudrow

HIGHEST-PAID TV ACTRESSES

Money earned per episode

Jennifer Aniston, *Friends*	Courteney Cox Arquette, *Friends*	Lisa Kudrow, *Friends*	Jane Leeves, *Frasier*	Paricia Heaton, *Everybody Loves Raymond*
$1.0 M	$1.0 M	$1.0 M	$450,000	$250,000

Highest-Paid TV Actor

Ray Romano

Ray Romano became the highest-paid actor on television in 2003, earning $50 million for the 2004 season of *Everybody Loves Raymond*. This brings his per-episode salary up to between $1.7 and $1.8 million dollars—more than double his $800,000 salary of the previous season. Romano recently picked up his first Emmy Award for Lead Actor in a Comedy Series in 2002. The show, which enters its eighth season on CBS, also stars Patricia Heaton, Doris Roberts, Peter Boyle, and Brad Garrett.

HIGHEST-PAID TV ACTORS

Money earned per episode in millions of US dollars

$1.75 M	$1.60 M	$1.00 M	$1.00 M	$1.00 M
Ray Romano, *Everybody Loves Raymond*	Kelsey Grammer, *Frasier*	Matt LeBlanc, *Friends*	Matthew Perry, *Friends*	David Schwimmer, *Friends*

Most Emmy® Awards
In a Single Season

The West Wing

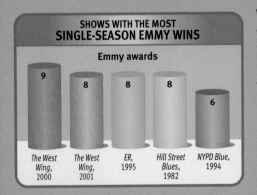

SHOWS WITH THE MOST
SINGLE-SEASON EMMY WINS

Emmy awards

The West Wing, 2000	The West Wing, 2001	ER, 1995	Hill Street Blues, 1982	NYPD Blue, 1994
9	8	8	8	6

The West Wing—an NBC drama about life in the White House—won a record-setting nine awards at the 52nd Primetime Emmy® Awards in September 2000. Some of the awards won that night included Outstanding Drama Series, Best Supporting Actor, and Best Supporting Actress. The cast of *The West Wing* includes many distinguished actors, including Martin Sheen as President Josiah Bartlet, John Spencer as Chief of Staff Leo McGarry, Bradley Whitford as Deputy Chief of Staff Josh Lyman, and Stockard Channing as First Lady Abby Bartlet. Allison Janney, who plays Press Secretary C.J. Cregg, earned two Emmy® Awards in 2000 and 2001. *The West Wing* has also won a Peabody Award, a Golden Globe, and several Television Critics Association Awards.

Actor with the Highest Career
Box-Office Earnings

Harrison Ford has appeared in more than twenty-five films and leads all other actors in total box-office earnings with more than $3 billion dollars. To date, ten of his movies have grossed more than $200 million each, and fifteen have earned more than $100 million each. Ford's biggest moneymaker so far has been *Star Wars*, which was released in 1977. The action film has earned more than $798 million worldwide. Some of Ford's other popular movies include *Raiders of the Lost Ark* (1981), *The Empire Strikes Back* (1980), *Patriot Games* (1992), and *Air Force One* (1997). For recent films, Ford's salary has averaged about $20 million per picture.

ACTORS WITH THE HIGHEST
CAREER BOX-OFFICE EARNINGS

Earnings in billions
of US dollars

Harrison Ford	Tom Hanks	Tom Cruise	Mel Gibson	Jim Carrey
$3.01 B	$2.52 B	$2.28 B	$1.83 B	$1.49 B

Harrison
Ford

World's Highest Paid
Actress

Julia Roberts

American superstar Julia Roberts was paid a record-breaking $20 million to portray a working single mom in the 2000 box-office hit *Erin Brockovich*, which won her an Academy Award® for Best Actress. She earned the same salary the following year for her role in *The Mexican* with Brad Pitt. Roberts made her professional film debut in 1988 in the movie *Mystic Pizza*. She has also received Oscar® nominations for her roles in *Steel Magnolias* and *Pretty Woman*. Some of Roberts's other well-known movies include *Ocean's Eleven*, *Runaway Bride*, *America's Sweethearts* and *Mona Lisa Smile*.

20

THE WORLD'S
HIGHEST-PAID ACTRESSES

Approximate salary per movie, in millions of US dollars

$20.0 M	$20.0 M	$17.5 M	$15.0 M	$15.0 M
Julia Roberts, *The Mexican* 2001	Julia Roberts, *Erin Brockovich* 2000	Cameron Diaz, *Gangs of New York* 2002	Julia Roberts, *Runaway Bride* 1999	Reese Witherspoon, *Legally Blond 2* 2003

World's Highest-Paid Actor

Arnold Schwarzenegger earned a record-shattering $30 million for his role as T-850 in *Terminator 3: Rise of the Machines* in 2003. In the third installment of the sci-fi action movie saga that began in 1984, he reprises his role as the Terminator. Schwarzenegger's first title role in a movie was *Conan the Barbarian* in 1982 for which he earned $250,000. In 1996, Schwarzenegger earned $20 million for *Jingle All the Way*. By the late 1990s, his salary had increased to $25 million for movies such as *Batman and Robin* (1997), *End of Days* (1999) and *The 6th Day* (2000). Besides acting, Schwarzenegger has also helped to produce some of his movies, in addition to directing some television productions.

THE WORLD'S HIGHEST-PAID ACTORS

Salary in millions of US dollars

$30 M	$25 M	$25 M	$25 M	$22.5 M
Arnold Schwarzenegger, *Terminator 3*, 2003	Tom Cruise, *Minority Report*, 2002	Mel Gibson, *Signs*, 2002	Arnold Schwarzenegger, *The 6th Day*, 2000	Bruce Willis, *Hart's War*, 2002

Arnold Schwarzenegger

Actor with the Most
MTV Movie Awards

Jim Carrey

Jim Carrey has picked up nine MTV Movie Awards since the network began the ceremony in 1992. He has won four awards for Best Comedic Performance (*Dumb and Dumber*—1994; *Ace Ventura: When Nature Calls*—1995; *The Cable Guy*—1996; *Liar Liar*—1997). He picked up one award for Best Kiss (*Dumb and Dumber*). Carrey won Best Male Performance for *Ace Ventura: When Nature Calls* and *The Truman Show*—1998. He also earned two awards for Best Villain in *The Cable Guy* and *How the Grinch Stole Christmas*—2000.

ACTORS WITH THE
MOST MTV MOVIE AWARDS

Number of awards

Jim Carrey	Mike Myers	Keanu Reeves	Adam Sandler	Will Smith
9	5	4	4	4

Actress with the Most
MTV Movie Awards

Alicia Silverstone

Alicia Silverstone has won four MTV Movie Awards—more than any other actress. She earned two awards—Best Villain and Best Breakthrough Performance—for her work on the 1993 movie *The Crush* when she was just 15 years old. Her next two awards—Most Desirable Female and Best Female Performance—came for the popular 1995 comedy *Clueless*. MTV viewers also know Silverstone from her appearances in several Aerosmith videos. MTV, which awards actors and actresses based on viewers' votes, is known for its offbeat award categories.

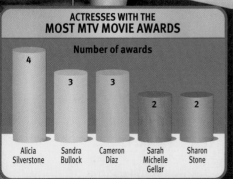

ACTRESSES WITH THE MOST MTV MOVIE AWARDS

Number of awards

Alicia Silverstone	Sandra Bullock	Cameron Diaz	Sarah Michelle Gellar	Sharon Stone
4	3	3	2	2

World's Largest Pre-Approved Movie Budget

Terminator 3

Terminator 3: The Rise of the Machines had an approved budget of $170 million. Although other movies had budgets that ultimately grew much higher during production, this is the first movie to get the go-ahead for such a large budget before the movie even started filming. *Terminator 3* opened in July 2003 starring Arnold Schwarzenegger as the Terminator, Nick Stahl as John Connor, and Kristanna Loken as T-X. In the movie, the Terminator returns to save Connor from T-X, a sophisticated cyborg-killing machine. The original *Terminator* was released in 1984, and the sequel, *Terminator 2: Judgment Day,* came out in 1991.

THE WORLD'S LARGEST
PRE-APPROVED MOVIE BUDGETS

Pre-approved budget
in millions of US dollars

$170 M	$140 M	$135 M	$125 M	$100 M
Terminator 3 2003	Armageddon 1998	Pearl Harbor 2001	Titanic 1997	Planet of the Apes 2001

Most Successful Movie
Opening Weekend

Spider-Man

MOVIES WITH THE BEST OPENING WEEKENDS

Weekend earnings in millions of US dollars

$114.8 M	$91.7 M	$90.3 M	$88.4 M	$85.5 M
Spider-Man 5/3/02	The Matrix Reloaded 5/15/03	Harry Potter and the Sorcerer's Stone 11/16/01	Harry Potter and the Chamber of Secrets 11/15/02	X2: X-Men United 5/4/03

On the first weekend in May 2002, the comic book thriller *Spider-Man* earned an amazing $114.8 million. The box-office receipts from this one weekend made up more than a quarter of the film's total gross of $404 million. The Sony film—which opened in more than 3,600 movie theaters across the country—starred Tobey Maguire as Spider-Man and Kirsten Dunst as his love interest, Mary Jane Watson. Willem Dafoe played the movie's villain—the Green Goblin.

World's Top-Grossing Kids' Movie

Snow White and the Seven Dwarfs

In the 67 years since its debut, Walt Disney's *Snow White and the Seven Dwarfs* has earned an amazing $1.03 billion in box office receipts to date. (To compare the success of films throughout the decades, it is necessary to adjust for inflation.) More than 750 artists were used during the three-year production. *Snow White and the Seven Dwarfs* was the first-ever animated feature film, and it cost $1.4 million to make. Many of the songs in the movie, including "Some Day My Prince Will Come" and "Whistle While You Work," have become true American classics.

THE WORLD'S TOP-GROSSING KIDS' MOVIES

Box office receipts in billions and millions of constant dollars

$1.03 B	$975 M	$865 M	$798 M	$788 M
Snow White and the Seven Dwarfs	Harry Potter and the Sorceror's Stone	Harry Potter and the Chamber of Secrets	Star Wars	The Lion King

World's Top-Grossing Movie

Titanic

The blockbuster movie *Titanic* has grossed more than $600 million in the United States and more than $1.8 billion worldwide. Directed by James Cameron in 1998, this action-packed drama/romance is set aboard the White Star Line's lavish *RMS Titanic* in 1912. The two main characters, wealthy Rose DeWitt Bukater and the poor immigrant, Jack Dawson—played by Kate Winslet and Leonardo DiCaprio—meet, fall in love, and are separated as the *Titanic* sinks into the North Atlantic on the morning of April 15, 1912.

THE WORLD'S TOP-GROSSING MOVIES

Gross income in billions and millions of US dollars

$1.83 B				
	$975 M	$925 M	$920 M	$918 M
Titanic, 1998	Harry Potter and the Sorceror's Stone, 2001	Phantom Menace, 1999	Jurassic Park, 1993	The Two Towers, 2002

Movie with the Most Oscars®

Ben-Hur/ Titanic

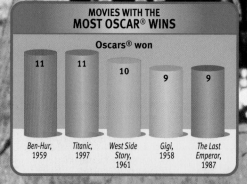

MOVIES WITH THE MOST OSCAR® WINS

Oscars® won

Ben-Hur, 1959	Titanic, 1997	West Side Story, 1961	Gigi, 1958	The Last Emperor, 1987
11	11	10	9	9

The only two films in Hollywood history to win 11 Academy Awards are *Ben-Hur* and *Titanic*. *Ben-Hur*—a Biblical epic that was released in 1959—is based on an 1880 novel by General Lew Wallace. The screen adaptation cost $15 million to produce, making *Ben-Hur* the most expensive film of its time. Charlton Heston, who played the hero, won the only Oscar® of his career for this movie. Some other Oscars® included Best Picture, Best Supporting Actor (Hugh Griffith), and Best Score. Some of *Titanic's* wins included Best Picture and Best Director (James Cameron).

Ben-Hur

Country That Makes the Most Movies

India

Filmmakers in India produce an average of 855 movies annually. With that availability, it's not surprising that movies have replaced theater as the favorite national pastime of India. Bombay (Mumbai) has earned the nickname "Bollywood," for its Hollywood-like productions. But many Indian movies also enjoy a worldwide audience. In 2002, *Lagaan* became the third Indian movie ever to be nominated for an Academy Award® for Best Foreign Film. *Monsoon Wedding*, by New York–based Indian director Mira Nair, was also a hit with U.S. audiences in 2001 and received a Golden Globe nomination.

COUNTRIES THAT PRODUCE THE MOST MOVIES

Average number of movies produced each year

India	USA	Japan	Hong Kong	France
855	762	282	185	171

World's Longest-Running Broadway Show

Cats

Since its debut, the cast of the Broadway hit *Cats* performed 7,485 shows. That means they averaged one show each day for almost 19 years! The show began at The New London Theater in England in May 1981 and later opened at the Winter Garden on Broadway in October 1982. This tale about the "jellicle cats" had 2,500 props built into its set and used more than 100 props on stage. There were about 250 different costumes and more than 35 wigs made from yak hair. The show has been seen by more than 50 million people worldwide and has grossed more than $2 billion. *Cats* closed in September 2000.

THE WORLD'S LONGEST-RUNNING BROADWAY SHOWS

Total performances*

Cats, 1982–2000	Les Misérables, 1987–	Phantom of the Opera, 1988–	A Chorus Line, 1975–1990	Oh! Calcutta!, 1969–1972
7,485	6,680	6,414	6,137	5,959

*As of June 16, 2003

Play with the Most Tony Awards

The Producers

The Producers took home twelve of its record-breaking fifteen Tony nominations in March 2001. The Broadway smash took home awards for Best Musical, Best Original Score, Best Book, Best Direction of a Musical, Best Choreography, Best Orchestration, Best Scenic Design, Best Costume Design, Best Lighting Design, Best Actor in a Musical, Best Featured Actor in a Musical, and Best Actress in a Musical. *The Producers*, which starred Nathan Lane and Matthew Broderick, is a stage adaptation of Mel Brooks' 1968

PLAYS WITH THE MOST TONY AWARDS

Number of Tony awards

The Producers, 2001	Hello Dolly, 1964	Thoroughly Modern Millie, 2002	A Man for All Seasons, 1962	The Real Thing, 1984
12	10	6	5	5

Most Valuable Auctioned
Painting

Portrait of Dr. Gachet

The Portrait of Dr. Gachet, an oil painting by Dutch Impressionist Vincent van Gogh, was sold to Ryoei Saito at a Christie's auction in 1990 for $82.5 million. Soon after the painting was purchased, it was locked away in a special vault for safekeeping. However, since Saito's death in 1996, the painting's location has remained a mystery. The painting's subject, Dr. Gachet, lived from 1828 to 1909 and specialized in homeopathy. The doctor loved the arts and supported several famous artists. In May of 1890, Gachet invited van Gogh to stay with him at Auvers-sur-Oise in France. There, van Gogh painted 70 canvases in just 70 days.

THE WORLD'S MOST VALUABLE
PAINTINGS SOLD AT AUCTION

Price in millions of US dollars

$82.5 M	$76.7 M	$71.0 M	$65.0 M	$55.0 M
Portrait of Dr. Gachet, van Gogh	The Massacre of the Innocents, Peter Paul Rubens	Au Moulin de la Galette, Pierre-Auguste Renoir	Portrait de l'Artiste Sans Barbe, van Gogh	Rideau, Cruchon et Compotier, Paul Cézanne

World's Most Expensive Painting
By a Woman Artist

The Conversation

THE WORLD'S MOST EXPENSIVE
WOMEN'S PAINTINGS SOLD AT AUCTION

Price paid in millions of US dollars

$4.1 M	$4.0 M	$3.7 M	$3.5 M	$3.5 M
The Conversation, Mary Cassatt	Cache-cache, Berthe Morisot	In the Box, Mary Cassatt	Cache-cache, Berthe Morisot	Mother, Sara and the Baby, Mary Cassatt

On May 11, 1988, Mary Cassatt's oil painting *The Conversation* sold for $4.1 million at a Christie's auction and is now part of a private collection. Similar to *The Conversation*, the majority of Cassatt's paintings and pastel sketches feature women and children participating in everyday activities. Cassatt studied at the Pennsylvania Academy of Fine Arts before studying art in Europe in 1865. After settling in Paris, she began to work with acclaimed Impressionists Edouard Manet and Edgar Degas. Cassatt was greatly influenced by both their subjects and their techniques.

Science and Technology Records

Vehicles • Technology • Computers
Video Games • Space • Solar System

World's Fastest Production
Motorcycle

Suzuki GSX1300R Hayabusa

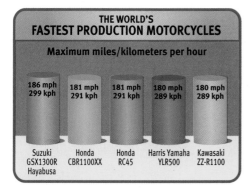

THE WORLD'S
FASTEST PRODUCTION MOTORCYCLES

Maximum miles/kilometers per hour

186 mph 299 kph	181 mph 291 kph	181 mph 291 kph	180 mph 289 kph	180 mph 289 kph
Suzuki GSX1300R Hayabusa	Honda CBR1100XX	Honda RC45	Harris Yamaha YLR500	Kawasaki ZZ-R1100

This sleek speed machine, which is named after one of the world's fastest birds, is able to reach a maximum speed of 186 miles (299 km) per hour. That's about three times faster than the speed limit on most major highways. In 1999, the Hayabusa won several major awards, including Motorcycle of the Year and Best Superbike. Its aerodynamic shape, four-cylinder liquid-cooled engine, six-speed transmission, and powerful disc brakes make the bike very popular with motorcycle enthusiasts. The Hayabusa sells for about $11,000.

World's Fastest
Production Car

McLaren F1

THE WORLD'S FASTEST PRODUCTION CARS

Maximum miles/kilometers per hour

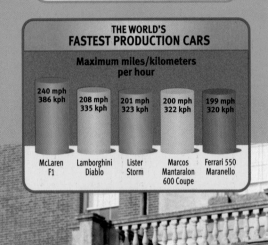

McLaren F1	Lamborghini Diablo	Lister Storm	Marcos Mantaralon 600 Coupe	Ferrari 550 Maranello
240 mph 386 kph	208 mph 335 kph	201 mph 323 kph	200 mph 322 kph	199 mph 320 kph

In March of 1998, a McLaren F1 driven by Andy Wallace reached a top speed of 240 miles (386 km) per hour, making it the fastest production (mass-produced) car in history. It can accelerate from 0–60 miles (96 km) per hour in just 3.2 seconds and cover a quarter of a mile in just over 11 seconds. The car is made mostly of light carbon fiber, which means the McLaren only weighs a total of 2,509 pounds (1,138 kg). The 48-valve V-12 engine by BMW produces an amazing 627 horsepower. The McLaren also has a six-speed transmission and independent suspension. The car was manufactured from 1993 to 1998, but the company only produced 100 cars.

World's
Largest Yacht

Abdul Aziz

THE WORLD'S
LARGEST YACHTS

Length in feet/meters

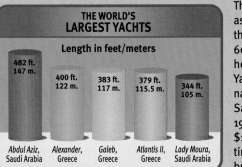

482 ft. 147 m.	400 ft. 122 m.	383 ft. 117 m.	379 ft. 115.5 m.	344 ft. 105 m.
Abdul Aziz, Saudi Arabia	Alexander, Greece	Galeb, Greece	Atlantis II, Greece	Lady Moura, Saudi Arabia

The largest yacht in the world measures an astounding 482 feet (147 m) long—about half the length of a commercial ocean liner! It features 60 guest rooms, two swimming pools, and a helicopter pad. It was built in the Vospers Ship Yard in England in 1984. This royal yacht was named after its owner, Prince Abdul Aziz of Saudi Arabia. When he acquired the yacht in 1987, it was estimated to be worth more than $100 million in U.S. currency. At the time, the prince was just 18 years old, but was already worth about $1 billion.

World's Fastest Land Vehicle

Thrust SSC

The Thrust SSC, which stands for SuperSonic Car, reached a speed of 763 miles (1,228 km) per hour on October 15, 1997. At that speed, a car could make it from San Francisco to New York City in less than 4 hours. The Thrust SSC is propelled by two jet engines capable of 110,000 horsepower. The Thrust SSC runs on jet fuel, using about 5 gallons (19 l) per second. It only takes approximately five seconds for this supersonic car to reach its top speed. It is 54 feet (16.5 m) long and weighs 7 tons (6.4 t)

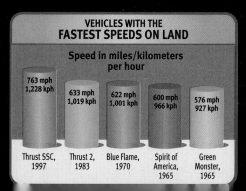

VEHICLES WITH THE FASTEST SPEEDS ON LAND

Speed in miles/kilometers per hour

763 mph 1,228 kph	633 mph 1,019 kph	622 mph 1,001 kph	600 mph 966 kph	576 mph 927 kph
Thrust SSC, 1997	Thrust 2, 1983	Blue Flame, 1970	Spirit of America, 1965	Green Monster, 1965

World's Largest
Cruise Ships

Adventure of the Seas, Explorer of the Seas, Voyager of the Seas

The *Adventure of the Seas*, the *Explorer of the Seas*, and the *Voyager of the Seas* are luxury cruise ships that each weigh 156,526 tons (142,000 t) or 313 million pounds (142 million kg). Each of these Royal Caribbean ships measures 1,024 feet (312 m) long and can carry up to 3,114 passengers and 1,181 crew. That's larger than most hotels. All of these ships depart from Miami and cruise to various islands in the western Caribbean. While at sea, guests can go ice skating, swim in three pools, try the rock climbing wall, or stroll through the street fair.

THE WORLD'S LARGEST CRUISE SHIPS

Gross tonnage

Voyager of the Seas	Adventure of the Seas	Explorer of the Seas	Navigator of the Seas	Grand Princess
156,526 tn. 142,000 t.	156,526 tn. 142,000 t.	156,526 tn. 142,000 t.	119,936 tn. 108,806 t.	119,936 tn. 108,806 t.

World's Fastest
Plane

The Lockheed SR-71 Blackbird flew at a top speed of 2,193 miles (3,529 km) per hour. At that rate, the Blackbird could fly from Los Angeles to New York City in just 90 minutes instead of the average commercial jetliner time of 6 hours. This super speedy plane also holds the record for flying at the highest altitude, which is 85,069 feet (25,929 m). Manufactured in the United States, this two-seater plane was used by the military from 1966 to 1999. The Blackbird measures 107.5 feet (32.8 m) long and has a wingspan of 55.7 feet (17 m).

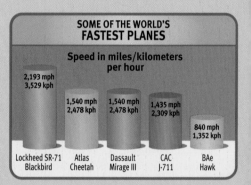

SOME OF THE WORLD'S FASTEST PLANES

Speed in miles/kilometers per hour

2,193 mph 3,529 kph	1,540 mph 2,478 kph	1,540 mph 2,478 kph	1,435 mph 2,309 kph	840 mph 1,352 kph
Lockheed SR-71 Blackbird	Atlas Cheetah	Dassault Mirage III	CAC J-711	BAe Hawk

World's Fastest
Roller Coaster

Dodonpa

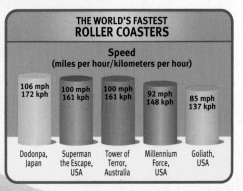

THE WORLD'S FASTEST
ROLLER COASTERS

Speed
(miles per hour/kilometers per hour)

Dodonpa, Japan	Superman the Escape, USA	Tower of Terror, Australia	Millennium Force, USA	Goliath, USA
106 mph 172 kph	100 mph 161 kph	100 mph 161 kph	92 mph 148 kph	85 mph 137 kph

Flying down the rails at a heart-stopping 106 miles (172 km) per hour, Dodonpa is the fastest roller coaster in the world. Located in Fujikyu Highland, about 60 miles (97 km) from Tokyo, Japan, Dodonpa can reach top speed in just 2 seconds. This amazing burst of power lets riders experience a G force of 3.6—usually only experienced by fighter pilots. In fact, Dodonpa features the wheels of a small airplane, but has 50,000 horsepower, which is comparable to a small rocket. The track is .75 mile long (1.2 km) and features a 169-foot (52 m) near-vertical drop and a 74-degree bend. The ride lasts about a minute and costs 1,000 yen—about $8 in American money.

World's Biggest
Monster Truck

The Bigfoot 5 truly is a monster—it measures 15.4 feet (4.7 m) high! That's about three times the height of an average car. Bigfoot 5 has 10-foot (3-m) high Firestone Tundra tires each weighing 2,400 pounds (1,088 kg), giving the truck a total weight of about 38,000 pounds (17,236 kg). This modified 1996 Ford F250 pickup truck is owned by Bob Chandler of St. Louis, Missouri. The great weight of this monster truck makes it too large to race, but several other trucks in Chandler's "Bigfoot" series are quite successful in monster truck championships.

Bigfoot 5

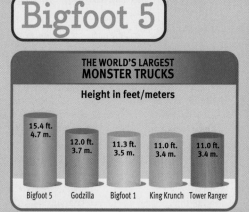

THE WORLD'S LARGEST MONSTER TRUCKS

Height in feet/meters

Bigfoot 5	Godzilla	Bigfoot 1	King Krunch	Tower Ranger
15.4 ft. 4.7 m.	12.0 ft. 3.7 m.	11.3 ft. 3.5 m.	11.0 ft. 3.4 m.	11.0 ft. 3.4 m.

World's Fastest
Passenger Train

Nozomi

The Nozomi carries passengers in Japan from Hiroshima to Kokura at an average speed of 162 miles (261 km) per hour. At that speed, the 119-mile (192-km) train ride takes only 44 minutes. The Nozomi also carries passengers for 370 miles (595 km) on the Sanyo Line between Osaka and Hakata, arriving at the station in just 2 hours and 17 minutes. The train is capable of reaching a maximum speed of 186 miles (299 km) per hour. This train was designed by the West Japan Railway Company and is part of the Japanese 500 design series.

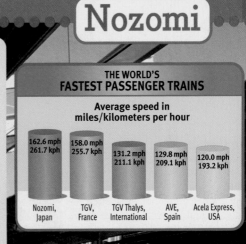

**THE WORLD'S
FASTEST PASSENGER TRAINS**

**Average speed in
miles/kilometers per hour**

162.6 mph 261.7 kph	158.0 mph 255.7 kph	131.2 mph 211.1 kph	129.8 mph 209.1 kph	120.0 mph 193.2 kph
Nozomi, Japan	TGV, France	TGV Thalys, International	AVE, Spain	Acela Express, USA

Country with the
Most Telephones

Sweden

The phone companies in Sweden must be pretty busy. For every 10 people living in the country, there are 7 telephones. That is five times higher than the world average. It means that the country's 8.9 million Swedish residents have access to more than 6.0 million telephones. Sweden's capital, Stockholm, has the highest concentration of telephones. That's not too surprising because the city is a world leader in the production of communications equipment. Sweden also has excellent domestic and international telephone systems.

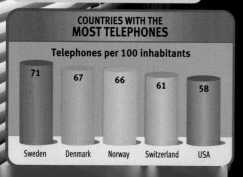

**COUNTRIES WITH THE
MOST TELEPHONES**

Telephones per 100 inhabitants

Sweden	Denmark	Norway	Switzerland	USA
71	67	66	61	58

Country with the Most
Cell Phone Users

Finland

In Finland, about 75% of the population is taking advantage of wireless communication. There are 75 cell phone users per every 100 people. The country is one of the most northern and geographically remote in the world. Reliable communication in Finland is very important for its people. Finland is also a leader in the development of wireless technology. Many popular cell phone brands, such as Nokia—the world's leading mobile phone supplier—originated in Finland.

COUNTRIES WITH THE
MOST CELL PHONE USERS

Cell phone users per 100 people

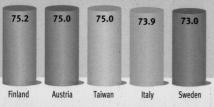

Finland	Austria	Taiwan	Italy	Sweden
75.2	75.0	75.0	73.9	73.0

Country with the
Most TV Sets

United States

There are approximately 844 television sets for every 1,000 people in the United States. That means there are about 243 million U.S. televisions in use right now. Approximately 67% of television owners subscribe to basic cable, which means nearly 70 million viewers have access to a wide range of channels. Americans have become addicted to television. The average person living in the United States watches about 1,551 hours of television programming each year. That's equal to nearly 65 straight days, or 18% of one year.

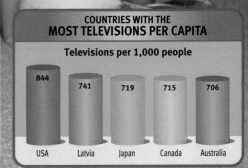

COUNTRIES WITH THE
MOST TELEVISIONS PER CAPITA

Televisions per 1,000 people

USA	Latvia	Japan	Canada	Australia
844	741	719	715	706

World's Highest
Internet Use

Canada

COUNTRIES WITH THE
HIGHEST PER CAPITA INTERNET USE

Internet users per 1,000 inhabitants

Canada	Sweden	Finland	USA	Iceland
428	414	408	406	403

Canada has a per capita Internet usage rate of 428 per 1,000 residents. That means that about 43% of the country—some 18.5 million people—are connected to the Internet. Users go on-line to shop, play games, do research, and learn. Canada has a strong education system—in fact, it is ranked first in the world by the United Nations. Canada's population has a literacy rate of 97%.

47

Country with the Most
Internet Users

The United States

In the United States, more than 160 million people are surfing the World Wide Web. That's about 50% of the population. The top five on-line activities in 2002 were email and instant messaging, Web surfing, reading news, shopping, and accessing entertainment information. Throughout the nation, the largest number of Internet users is women between the ages of 18 and 54, closely followed by men in that age group. Teens ages 12 to 17 are the third-largest Internet-using group. The average Internet user spends about 11 hours on-line per week.

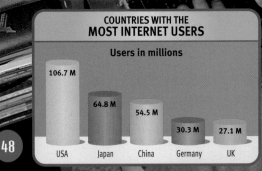

COUNTRIES WITH THE MOST INTERNET USERS

Users in millions

106.7 M	64.8 M	54.5 M	30.3 M	27.1 M
USA	Japan	China	Germany	UK

World's Most-Visited Web Site

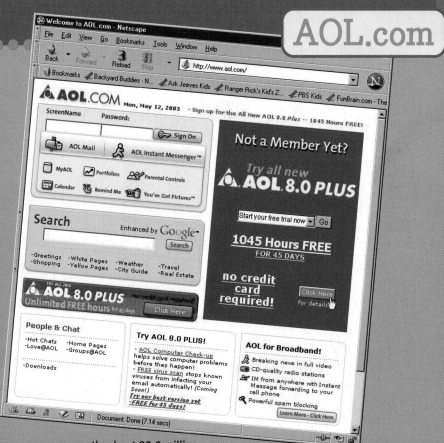

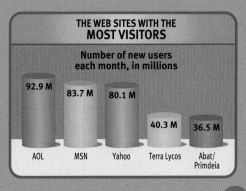

During an average month, about 92.9 million Internet users visit the AOL Web site at least once. AOL became one of the most popular Internet service providers when it debuted 18 years ago. Since that time, the company has grown to employ 19,000 people and serve 35 million members worldwide. It processes about 400 million e-mails and 2.1 billion instant messages each day. Every day each member spends an average of 70 minutes on-line and visits some of the 13.4 billion Web URLs processed daily. Some of the Web sites in the AOL family include ICQ, MapQuest, Moviefone, Netscape, and Winamp & Spinner.

THE WEB SITES WITH THE MOST VISITORS

Number of new users each month, in millions

AOL	MSN	Yahoo	Terra Lycos	Abat/Primdeia
92.9 M	83.7 M	80.1 M	40.3 M	36.5 M

World's Most-Used Internet Search Engine

Yahoo!

Yahoo! is the most-used Internet search engine and reaches some 65% of computer users each year. Founded in 1994 by Stanford students Jerry Yang and David Filo, Yahoo stands for Yet Another Hierarchical Office Oracle. The Web site reaches users in 25 countries and is offered in 13 different languages. In addition to its comprehensive searching services, the site also offers Yahoo! Mail, Yahoo! Chat, Yahoo! Messenger, and Yahoo! Photos to help Web surfers stay in touch. Some of the other companies that Yahoo! owns include HotJobs, MyQuest, Broadcast.com, and ViaWeb.

MOST-USED INTERNET SEARCH ENGINES

Percentage of total users

Yahoo!	MSN	Lycos	Go.com	Google
65%	58%	45%	29%	24%

Country with the Most
Computers-in-Use

The United States

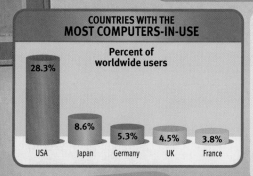

COUNTRIES WITH THE MOST COMPUTERS-IN-USE

Percent of worldwide users

Country	Percent
USA	28.3%
Japan	8.6%
Germany	5.3%
UK	4.5%
France	3.8%

The United States is computer crazy—more than one-quarter of the world's computer users live here! There are about 185 million computers in the United States. Americans use computers for business and school, to pay bills, send e-mail, and play games. Surfing the World Wide Web is also a popular American pastime. In the next few years, there will be 57 million households connected to the Internet. Many Americans are also shopping on-line and will spend an estimated $36 billion in 2003.

Video Games

World's Best-Selling
Kid's Video Game

Super Mario
Advance 2

ONLY FOR

GAME BOY ADVANCE

SUPER MARIO WORLD
SUPER MARIO ADVANCE 2

Link It Up!
1 Game Pak
4 Players
See back panel for details.

WITH CLASSIC MARIO BROS. ARCADE—INCLUDED!

EVERYONE
E
CONTENT RATED BY ESRB

Nintendo

Super Mario Advance 2 was the most popular kid's video game in 2002, selling 4.8 million copies. Nintendo's latest Super Mario Bros. adventure takes place as the brothers are planning a vacation on Dinosaur Island. But before they leave, they find out that Princess Peach has been kidnapped and they must fight off the evil Bowser to rescue her. While exploring the game's 74 different levels, players can use Mario and Luigi's special powers and ride Yoshi the dinosaur. While traveling on Yoshi, the game's heroes can scoop up their enemies, spit out fireballs, and carry special items.

52

THE WORLD'S
BEST-SELLING KID'S VIDEO GAMES

Units sold in 2002
in millions

4.8 M | 4.3 M | 3.8 M | 3.6 M | 3.1 M

Super Mario Advance 2 | Gran Turismo 3: A-Spec | Spider-Man: The Movie | Kingdom Hearts | Super Mario Sunshine

World's Largest
Optical Telescopes

Keck I/Keck II

The Keck Observatory, located at the top of Mauna Kea in Hawaii, houses two giant optical telescopes—each with a 32.8-foot (10-m) aperture, or opening. Keck I was built in 1992, and Keck II was completed in 1996. Both telescopes stand 8 stories high and weigh 300 tons (272 t). Each telescope contains a primary mirror that measures 33 feet (10 m) in diameter. The telescopes are powerful enough to identify objects about the size of a penny at a distance of more than 5 miles (8 km) away. Astronomers use these giant machines to search for new planetary systems and study parts of the universe that were previously unobservable.

THE WORLD'S LARGEST OPTICAL TELESCOPES

Aperture in feet/meters

Keck I, Hawaii	Keck II, Hawaii	Hobby-Eberly, Texas	Subaru, Hawaii	Antu, Chile
32.8 ft. 10.0 m.	32.8 ft. 10.0 m.	30.1 ft. 9.2 m.	27.2 ft. 8.3 m.	26.9 ft. 8.2 m.

World's
Oldest Astronaut

John Glenn

At age 77, John Glenn returned to space on October 29, 1998 aboard the STS-95 *Discovery* on a nine-day mission. The mission made 134 Earth orbits and traveled 3.6 million miles (5.8 million km). One of the main parts of the mission was to study space flight and its affect on the aging process. Glenn took his first space flight in 1962 aboard the *Mercury-Atlas 6*. Since his first involvement with the space program, Glenn has been a colonel in the Marines and a U.S. Senator.

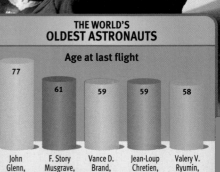

THE WORLD'S
OLDEST ASTRONAUTS

Age at last flight

John Glenn, USA	F. Story Musgrave, USA	Vance D. Brand, USA	Jean-Loup Chretien, France	Valery V. Ryumin, Russia
77	61	59	59	58

World's Youngest Astronaut

Gherman Titov became the youngest cosmonaut to travel into space when he made his only voyage on August 6, 1961, at the age of 25. Flying aboard the *Vostok 2* spacecraft, Titov completed 17.5 orbits, which lasted 1 day, 1 hour, and 18 minutes. During his time in space, he attempted several activities—including exercising, eating, and sleeping—which astronauts today do automatically. Once he returned to Earth, scientists studied the effects that weightlessness may have had on him.

Gherman Titov

THE WORLD'S YOUNGEST ASTRONAUTS

Age at first flight

Gherman S. Titov, Soviet Union	Valentina V. Tereshkova, Soviet Union	Boris B. Yegorov, Soviet Union	Yuri A. Gagarin, Soviet Union	Helen P. Sharman, Britain
25	26	26	27	27

Planet with the Hottest Surface

Venus

THE SOLAR SYSTEM'S
HOTTEST PLANETS

Average daytime temperature
in Fahrenheit/Celsius

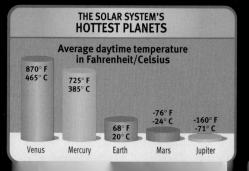

Venus	Mercury	Earth	Mars	Jupiter
870° F 465° C	725° F 385° C	68° F 20° C	-76° F -24° C	-160° F -71° C

The surface temperature on Venus can reach a sizzling 870° Fahrenheit (465° C). That's about 19 times hotter than the average temperature on Earth. About every 19 months, Venus is closer to Earth than any other planet in the solar system. Venus is covered by a cloudy, dense atmosphere. This cloud makes it difficult to know what features are on its surface. The atmosphere also reflects a great deal of sunlight. At times, Venus is the third-brightest object in the sky, after the Sun and the Moon.

Planet with the Most Rings

Saturn

Scientists estimate that approximately 1,000 r
circle Saturn—hundreds more than any other pl
This ring system is only about 328 feet (100 m
thick, but reaches a diameter of 167,780 miles
(270,000 km). The three major rings around th
planet are named A, B, and C. Although they
appear solid, Saturn's rings are made of particl
planet and satellite matter that range in size f
about 1 to 15 feet (.3 to 4.5 m). Saturn, which is
the sixth planet from the Sun, is the solar system
second-largest planet in size and mass.

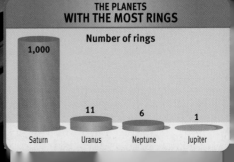

THE PLANETS WITH THE MOST RINGS

Number of rings

Saturn	Uranus	Neptune	Jupiter
1,000	11	6	1

Planet with the
Most Moons

Jupiter

Jupiter—the fifth planet from the Sun—has 58 moons. Most of these moons—also called satellites—do not resemble traditional moons. Most are quite small, measuring from just .62 miles (.99 km) to 4 miles (6.4 km) across. The moons travel in an elliptical, or egg-shaped, orbit in the opposite direction that Jupiter rotates. Astronomers believe these irregular moons formed somewhere else in the solar system and were pulled into Jupiter's atmosphere when they passed too close to the planet. Astronomers are constantly finding new moons for several of the planets, partly because of the highly sensitive telescopes and cameras now available to them.

THE PLANETS WITH THE
MOST MOONS

Number of moons

Jupiter	Saturn	Uranus	Neptune	Mars
58	31	21	11	2

Planet with the
Fastest Orbit

Mercury

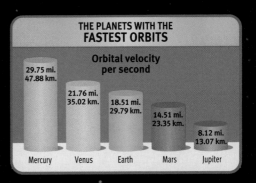

THE PLANETS WITH THE FASTEST ORBITS

Orbital velocity per second

Planet	Velocity
Mercury	29.75 mi. / 47.88 km.
Venus	21.76 mi. / 35.02 km.
Earth	18.51 mi. / 29.79 km.
Mars	14.51 mi. / 23.35 km.
Jupiter	8.12 mi. / 13.07 km.

Mercury orbits the Sun at about 30 miles (48 km) per second. At this astonishing speed, the planet can circle the Sun in about 88 Earth days. On Mercury, a solar day (the time from one sunrise to the next) lasts about 176 Earth days. Even though Mercury is the closest planet to the Sun, the temperature on the planet can change drastically. During the day, it can reach as high as 840° Fahrenheit (448° C), but at night, temperatures can fall to around -300° Fahrenheit (-149° C)!

Planet with the
Largest Moon

Jupiter

Ganymede is the largest moon of both Jupiter and the solar system. It has a radius of 1,635 miles (2,631 km) and a diameter of 3,280 miles (5,626 km). That is almost 2.5 times larger than Earth's moon. The moon is approximately 1.4 million miles (2.25 million km) away from Jupiter and has an orbital period of about seven days. It is probably made up mostly of rock and ice. It also has lava flows, mountains, valleys, and craters. Ganymede has both light and dark areas that give it a textured appearance. Ganymede was discovered by Galileo Galilei and Simon Marius almost 400 years ago.

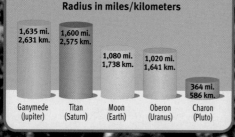

THE PLANETS WITH THE LARGEST MOONS

Radius in miles/kilometers

1,635 mi. 2,631 km.	1,600 mi. 2,575 km.	1,080 mi. 1,738 km.	1,020 mi. 1,641 km.	364 mi. 586 km.
Ganymede (Jupiter)	Titan (Saturn)	Moon (Earth)	Oberon (Uranus)	Charon (Pluto)

Star That is
Closest to Earth

Proxima Centauri

Proxima Centauri is approximately 24,792,500 miles (39,923,310 km) from Earth, making it our closest star other than the Sun. It is the third member of the Alpha Centauri triple system. This tiny red dwarf star is about 10% of the Sun's mass and .006% as bright. The surface temperature is thought to be about 3,000° Fahrenheit (1,650° C). More accurate measures of the star's size are not possible because it is so small. But these measurements are enough to cause scientists to believe that Proxima Centauri does not have any planets orbiting it that support life. If planets did exist, they would

THE STARS THAT ARE CLOSEST TO EARTH

Distance in millions of miles/kilometers

Proxima Centauri	Alpha Centauri	Barnard's Star	Wolf 359	Lalande 21185
24.8 M mi. 39.9 M km.	25.6 M mi. 41.2 M km.	35.1 M mi. 56.6 M km.	45.5 M mi. 73.3 M km.	48.3 M mi. 77.8 M km.

World's
Largest Asteroid

2001 KX76 is the largest asteroid in the universe, measuring at least 744 miles (1,200 km) long. The asteroid is about half the size of Pluto. 2001 KX76 is in the Kuiper belt of asteroids. It is about 4 billion miles (6.5 billion km) from Earth—or roughly 43 times the distance from Earth to the Sun. The asteroid was discovered by analyzing data from some of the world's most powerful virtual and conventional telescopes. Once astronomers were able to verify substantial data about the giant asteroid, it was accepted by the scientific community and is now eligible for a real name. Asteroids do not get permanent names until scientists can prove specific calculations of them. Asteroids in the Kuiper belt traditionally receive a mythological name.

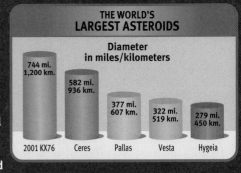

THE WORLD'S LARGEST ASTEROIDS

Diameter in miles/kilometers

Asteroid	Diameter
2001 KX76	744 mi. / 1,200 km.
Ceres	582 mi. / 936 km.
Pallas	377 mi. / 607 km.
Vesta	322 mi. / 519 km.
Hygeia	279 mi. / 450 km.

Planet with the Longest Year

Pluto

If you think a year on planet Earth is a long time, don't travel to Pluto any time soon! One year on Pluto is equivalent to 247.7 years on Earth, which means that a single day on Pluto is equal to 6.4 days on Earth. This is because Pluto's location ranges from 2.8 to 4.6 billion miles (4.4 to 7.4 billion km) away from the Sun, approximately 39 times farther from the Sun than Earth. Pluto is also the least massive planet in the solar system. Pluto's gravity is 8% of that on Earth, so that if a 75-pound (34-kg) kid were to be weighed on Pluto, he or she would weigh only 6 pounds (2.7 kg).

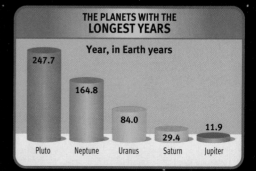

THE PLANETS WITH THE LONGEST YEARS

Year, in Earth years

Pluto	Neptune	Uranus	Saturn	Jupiter
247.7	164.8	84.0	29.4	11.9

Solar System's
Largest Planet

Jupiter

Jupiter has a radius of 43,441 miles (69,909 km)—that's almost 11 times larger than Earth's radius. Jupiter is about 480 million miles (772 million km) from the Sun. It takes almost 12 Earth years for Jupiter to make one complete circle around the Sun. Although it is very large, Jupiter has a high rotation speed. In fact, one Jupiter day is less than 10 Earth hours long. That is the shortest day in the solar system.

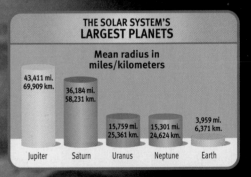

THE SOLAR SYSTEM'S
LARGEST PLANETS

Mean radius in
miles/kilometers

43,411 mi. 69,909 km.	36,184 mi. 58,231 km.	15,759 mi. 25,361 km.	15,301 mi. 24,624 km.	3,959 mi. 6,371 km.
Jupiter	Saturn	Uranus	Neptune	Earth

Solar System's
Smallest Planet

Pluto

Pluto has a radius of about 707 miles (1,138 km). That's about two-thirds the size of the Moon. Pluto is also the coldest planet, with an average surface temperature of -370° Fahrenheit (-233° Celsius). The planet appears to have polar ice caps that extend halfway to its equator. It is normally the farthest planet from the Sun, but its unusual orbit brings it closer than Neptune about every 250 years. The last time this happened was in 1979, when Pluto became the eighth planet for 20 years. First noticed in 1930, Pluto was the last planet to be discovered in our solar system.

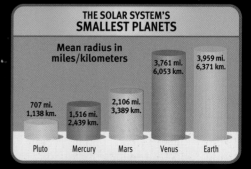

THE SOLAR SYSTEM'S SMALLEST PLANETS

Mean radius in miles/kilometers

707 mi. 1,138 km.	1,516 mi. 2,439 km.	2,106 mi. 3,389 km.	3,761 mi. 6,053 km.	3,959 mi. 6,371 km.
Pluto	Mercury	Mars	Venus	Earth

Sports Records

Football • Baseball • Basketball • Bicycling
Car Racing • Figure Skating • Tennis
Golf • Soccer • Olympics • Hockey

Highest Career
Rushing Total

Emmitt Smith

**PLAYERS WITH THE
HIGHEST CAREER RUSHING TOTALS**

Rushing yards

Emmitt Smith, 1990–	Walter Payton, 1975–1987	Barry Sanders, 1989–1999	Eric Dickerson, 1983–1993	Tony Dorsett, 1977–1988
17,162	16,726	15,269	13,259	12,739

Running back Emmitt Smith holds the record for all-time rushing yards with 17,126. Smith began his career with the Dallas Cowboys in 1990 and played with the team until the end of the 2002 season. In 2003, Smith signed a two-year contract with the Arizona Cardinals. Smith also holds the NFL records for the most carries with 4,052 and the most rushing touchdowns with 153.

67

Quarterback with the
Most Passing Yards

Dan Marino

During his seventeen-year career, Dan Marino has racked up 61,361 passing yards. Marino was selected by the Dolphins as the 27th pick in the first-round draft in 1983. He remained a Dolphin for the rest of his career, setting many impressive records. Marino has the most career pass attempts (8,358), the most career completions (4,967), the most career touchdown passes (420), the most passing yards in a season (5,084), and the most seasons leading the league in completions (6). Marino retired from the NFL in 2000.

PLAYERS WITH THE
MOST PASSING YARDS

Yards

Dan Marino 1983–2000	John Elway 1983–1999	Warren Moon 1984–2000	Fran Tarkenton 1961–1978	Dan Fouts 1973–1987
61,361	51,475	49,325	47,003	43,040

Most Single-Season Touchdowns

Marshall Faulk

Marshall Faulk scored a record 26 touchdowns for the St. Louis Rams during the 2000–2001 season. The San Diego State runningback was also named NFL MVP and Offensive Player of the Year that same season. He is one of only a few players to score four touchdowns in a game three times in one season, and to score more than 20 touchdowns in back-to-back seasons. Faulk has 110 career touchdowns and is ranked ninth in NFL history. Faulk began his career with the Indianapolis Colts and was later traded to the Rams in 1999. He has been selected for seven Pro Bowls in his nine-year career.

PLAYERS WITH THE MOST SINGLE-SEASON TOUCHDOWNS

Touchdowns scored

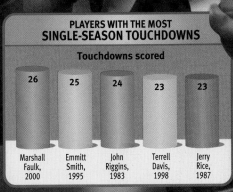

Marshall Faulk, 2000	Emmitt Smith, 1995	John Riggins, 1983	Terrell Davis, 1998	Jerry Rice, 1987
26	25	24	23	23

Most Career
Touchdowns

Jerry Rice

With a career record of 202 touchdowns, Jerry Rice is widely considered to be one of the greatest wide receivers ever to play in the National Football League. He holds a total of 14 NFL records, including career receptions (1,456), receiving yards (21,597), receiving touchdowns (192), consecutive 100-catch seasons (3), most games with 100 receiving yards (64), and many others. He was named NFL Player of the Year twice, *Sports Illustrated* Player of the Year four times, and NFL Offensive Player of the Year once.

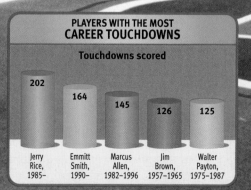

PLAYERS WITH THE MOST
CAREER TOUCHDOWNS

Touchdowns scored

Jerry Rice, 1985–	Emmitt Smith, 1990–	Marcus Allen, 1982–1996	Jim Brown, 1957–1965	Walter Payton, 1975–1987
202	164	145	126	125

Team with the Most
Super Bowl Wins

Cowboys and 49ers

The Dallas Cowboys and the San Francisco 49ers have each won a total of five Super Bowl championships. The first championship win for the Cowboys was in 1972, which was followed by wins in 1978, 1993, 1994, and 1996. Out of those 10 victories, the game with the most spectators was Super Bowl XXVII, when Dallas defeated the Buffalo Bills at the Rose Bowl in Pasadena, California, in 1993. The 49ers had their first win in 1982, and repeated their victory in 1985, 1989, 1990, and 1995.

TEAMS WITH THE MOST SUPER BOWL WINS

Super Bowls won

Dallas Cowboys	San Francisco 49ers	Pittsburgh Steelers	Green Bay Packers	Washington Redskins
5	5	4	3	3

Highest Career
Scoring Total

Gary Anderson

Gary Anderson is the Minnesota Vikings' top kicker. Altogether he has scored 2,223 points in his 20 seasons of professional play. He also holds several other NFL records, including postseason field goals made, with 28 in his career; field goals made, with 494 in his career; and career postseason scoring, with 143 points. In 1998, Anderson hit 35-of-35 field goals and became the first NFL player to go an entire season without missing a kick. Anderson began his career with the Pittsburgh Steelers in 1982 and has since played with the Philadelphia Eagles and the San Francisco 49ers. He joined the Vikings in 1998 and has scored 542 points for them— the fifth-highest in team history.

PLAYERS WITH THE
HIGHEST CAREER SCORING TOTALS

Points scored

Player	Points scored
Gary Anderson, 1982–	2,223
Morten Anderson, 1980–	2,153
George Blanda, 1949–1975	2,002
Norm Johnson, 1983–1999	1,736
Nick Lowery, 1978–1996	1,711

Biggest
Super Bowl Blowout

Super Bowl XXIV

On January 28, 1990, the San Francisco 49ers beat the Denver Broncos by a score of 55 to 10 during Super Bowl XXIV. Some 73,000 fans crowded into the Louisiana Superdome to see San Francisco score the most points in Super Bowl history. 49ers quarterback Joe Montana was named Super Bowl MVP for the third time, completing 22 out of 29 passes. San Francisco over-powered Denver in first downs (28 to 12) as well as net yards (461 to 167.)

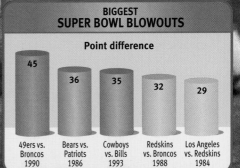

BIGGEST
SUPER BOWL BLOWOUTS

Point difference

45	36	35	32	29
49ers vs. Broncos 1990	Bears vs. Patriots 1986	Cowboys vs. Bills 1993	Redskins vs. Broncos 1988	Los Angeles vs. Redskins 1984

Top-Winning
NFL Coach

Don Shula

During his 33 years as a head coach in the National Football League, Don Shula led his teams to a remarkable 347 wins. When Shula became head coach of the Baltimore Colts in 1963, he became the youngest head coach in football history. He stayed with the team until 1969 and reached the playoffs four times. Shula became the head coach for the Miami Dolphins in 1970 and coached them until 1995. After leading them to Super Bowl wins in 1972 and 1973, Shula became one of only five coaches to win the championship in back-to-back years.

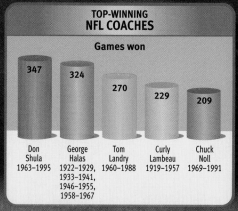

TOP-WINNING
NFL COACHES

Games won

347	324	270	229	209
Don Shula 1963–1995	George Halas 1922–1929, 1933–1941, 1946–1955, 1958–1967	Tom Landry 1960–1988	Curly Lambeau 1919–1957	Chuck Noll 1969–1991

Player Who Played the Most
Consecutive Games

Cal Ripken, Jr.

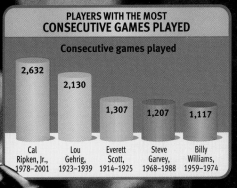

**PLAYERS WITH THE MOST
CONSECUTIVE GAMES PLAYED**

Consecutive games played

Cal Ripken, Jr., 1978–2001	Lou Gehrig, 1923–1939	Everett Scott, 1914–1925	Steve Garvey, 1968–1988	Billy Williams, 1959–1974
2,632	2,130	1,307	1,207	1,117

Cal Ripken, Jr., a right-handed third baseman for the Baltimore Orioles, played 2,632 consecutive games from May 30, 1982, to September 20, 1998. He also holds the record for the most consecutive innings played: 8,243. In June 1996, Ripken also broke the world record for consecutive games with 2,216, surpassing Sachio Kinugasa of Japan. When he played as a shortstop, Ripken set Major League records for most home runs (345) and most extra base hits (855) for his position. He has started in the All-Star Game a record 19 times in a row.

World's All-Time
Home Run Hitter

Hank Aaron

In 1974, Hank Aaron broke Babe Ruth's lifetime record of 714 home runs. By the time he retired from baseball in 1976, Aaron had hit a total of 755 homers—a record that has remained unbroken. His amazing hitting ability earned him the nickname "Hammerin' Hank." Aaron holds many other distinguished baseball records, including most lifetime runs batted in (2,297) and most years with 30 or more home runs (15). Aaron was an excellent defensive player, earning three Golden Glove Awards.

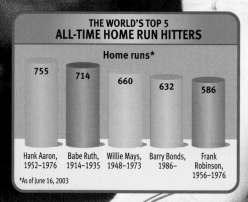

THE WORLD'S TOP 5
ALL-TIME HOME RUN HITTERS

Home runs*

755	714	660	632	586
Hank Aaron, 1952–1976	Babe Ruth, 1914–1935	Willie Mays, 1948–1973	Barry Bonds, 1986–	Frank Robinson, 1956–1976

*As of June 16, 2003

Highest Seasonal
Home Run Total

Barry Bonds

Highest Seasonal
Home Run Total

Barry Bonds

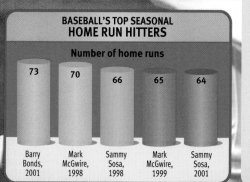

BASEBALL'S TOP SEASONAL HOME RUN HITTERS

Number of home runs

73	70	66	65	64
Barry Bonds, 2001	Mark McGwire, 1998	Sammy Sosa, 1998	Mark McGwire, 1999	Sammy Sosa, 2001

Barry Bonds smashed Mark McGwire's record for seasonal home runs when he hit his 71st home run on October 5, 2001, in the first inning of a game against the Los Angeles Dodgers. Two innings later, he hit number 72. Bonds, a left fielder for the San Francisco Giants, has a career total of 613 home runs. He also holds the records for seasonal walks (177) and seasonal slugging percentage (0.863). Bonds and his father, hitting coach Bobby Bonds, hold the all-time father-son home run record with 899.

Most
Career Hits

Pete Rose

During his 23 years of professional baseball, Rose belted an amazing 4,256 hits. He got his record-setting hit in 1985, when he was a player-manager for the Cincinnati Reds. By the time Pete Rose retired as a player from Major League Baseball in 1986, he had set several other career records. Rose holds the Major League records for the most career games (3,562), the most times at bat (14,053), and the most seasons with more than 200 hits (10). During his career, he played for the Cincinnati Reds, the Philadelphia Phillies, and the Montreal Expos.

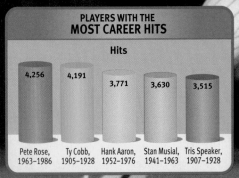

PLAYERS WITH THE
MOST CAREER HITS

Hits

Pete Rose, 1963–1986	Ty Cobb, 1905–1928	Hank Aaron, 1952–1976	Stan Musial, 1941–1963	Tris Speaker, 1907–1928
4,256	4,191	3,771	3,630	3,515

Most
Career Strikeouts

Nolan Ryan

Nolan Ryan, a right-handed pitcher from Refugio, Texas, leads Major League Baseball with an incredible 5,714 career strikeouts. In his impressive 28-year career, he played for the New York Mets, the California Angels, the Houston Astros, and the Texas Rangers. Ryan led the American League in strikeouts 10 times. In 1989, at the age of 42, Ryan became the oldest pitcher ever to lead the Major League in strikeouts. Ryan set another record in 1991 when he pitched his seventh career no-hitter.

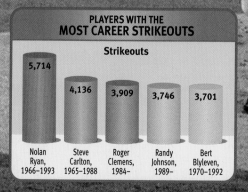

PLAYERS WITH THE
MOST CAREER STRIKEOUTS

Strikeouts

5,714	4,136	3,909	3,746	3,701
Nolan Ryan, 1966–1993	Steve Carlton, 1965–1988	Roger Clemens, 1984–	Randy Johnson, 1989–	Bert Blyleven, 1970–1992

Highest Seasonal
Batting Average

Rogers Hornsby

Rogers Hornsby is widely considered by most people to be Major League Baseball's greatest right-handed hitter. In 1924, he had a record-setting season batting average of .424. More than 75 years later, his record still stands. From 1921 to 1925—playing for the St. Louis Cardinals—Hornsby hit an average of .401. And during three of those seasons, he hit above .400. Hornsby's major league lifetime batting average is an incredible .358, which is the second-highest career average in the history of the league after Ty Cobb. Hornsby was inducted to the Baseball Hall of Fame in 1942.

PLAYERS WITH THE
HIGHEST SEASONAL BATTING AVERAGES

Season average

.424	.422	.420	.420	.410
Rogers Hornsby, 1924	Nap Lajoie, 1901	George Sisler, 1922	Ty Cobb, 1911	Ty Cobb, 1912

Baseball Player with the Most
Expensive Contract

In 2001, shortstop Alex Rodriguez signed a ten-year deal with the Texas Rangers for $25.2 million. This does not include any bonuses he may earn for winning titles or awards, or any money he could make from potential endorsements. The right-hander began his career with Seattle in 1994 and quickly became a respected player. He became the fourth shortstop ever to lead the league in home runs and is the second shortstop to ever be named player of the year by the Rangers.

Alex Rodriguez

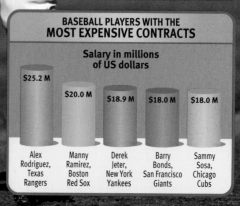

BASEBALL PLAYERS WITH THE
MOST EXPENSIVE CONTRACTS

Salary in millions
of US dollars

$25.2 M	$20.0 M	$18.9 M	$18.0 M	$18.0 M
Alex Rodriguez, Texas Rangers	Manny Ramirez, Boston Red Sox	Derek Jeter, New York Yankees	Barry Bonds, San Francisco Giants	Sammy Sosa, Chicago Cubs

Most MVP Awards in the National League

Barry Bonds

PLAYERS WITH THE MOST NATIONAL LEAGUE MVP AWARDS

Most Valuable Player (MVP) awards

Barry Bonds, 1986–	Roy Campanella, 1948–1957	Stan Musial, 1941–1963	Mike Schmidt, 1972–1989	Ernie Banks, 1953–1971
5	3	3	3	2

Barry Bonds of the San Francisco Giants has earned an amazing five Most Valuable Player awards for his outstanding athleticism in the National Baseball League. He received his first two MVP awards in 1990 and 1992 while playing for the Pittsburgh Pirates. The next three awards came while wearing the Giants uniform in 1993, 2001, and 2002. This pair of back-to-back wins also made Bonds the first player to win an MVP award twice in consecutive seasons. In fact, Bonds is the only baseball player in history to have won more than three MVP awards.

Most MVP Awards in the
American League

Yogi Berra, Joe DiMaggio, Jimmie Foxx, and Mickey Mantle each won three Most Valuable Player awards during their professional careers in the American Baseball League. DiMaggio, Berra, and Mantle were all New York Yankees. Foxx played for the Athletics, the Cubs, and the Phillies. The player with the biggest gap between wins was DiMaggio, who won his first award in 1939 and his last in 1947. Also nicknamed "Joltin' Joe" and the "Yankee Clipper," DiMaggio began playing in the major leagues in 1936. The following year, he led the league in home runs and runs scored. He was elected to the Baseball Hall of Fame in 1955.

Yogi Berra, Joe DiMaggio, Jimmie Foxx, and Mickey Mantle

PLAYERS WITH THE MOST
AMERICAN LEAGUE MVP AWARDS

Most Valuable Player (MVP) awards

Yogi Berra, 1946–1963; 1965	Joe DiMaggio, 1936–1951	Jimmie Foxx, 1925–1945	Mickey Mantle, 1951–1960	Juan Gonzalez, 1989–
3	3	3	3	2

Mickey Mantle

Most
Cy Young Awards

Roger Clemens

New York Yankees starting pitcher Roger Clemens has earned a record six Cy Young awards during his career so far. He set a Major League record in April of 1986 when he struck out 20 batters in one game. He later tied this record in September 1996. In September 2001, Clemens became the first Major League pitcher to win 20 of his first 21 decisions in one season. He has also earned an MVP award and two pitching Triple Crowns and has played in the All-Star Game eight times.

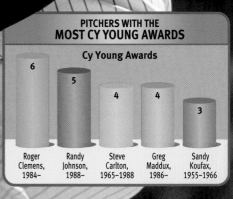

**PITCHERS WITH THE
MOST CY YOUNG AWARDS**

Cy Young Awards

6	5	4	4	3
Roger Clemens, 1984–	Randy Johnson, 1988–	Steve Carlton, 1965–1988	Greg Maddux, 1986–	Sandy Koufax, 1955–1966

Team with the Most
World Series Wins

New York Yankees

The New York Yankees were the World Series champions a record 26 times between 1923 and 2000. The team picked up their latest win in October of 2000 when they beat the New York Mets. The Yankees beat the Mets four games to one to win their third consecutive championship. Since their early days, the team has included some of baseball's greatest players, including Babe Ruth, Lou Gehrig, Yogi Berra, Joe DiMaggio, and Mickey Mantle.

TEAMS WITH THE MOST
WORLD SERIES WINS

Wins

26	9	9	6	5
NY Yankees, 1923–2000	St. Louis Cardinals, 1926–1982	Philadelphia/ Kansas City/ Oakland Athletics, 1910–1989	Brooklyn/ LA Dodgers, 1955–1988	NY/ San Francisco Giants, 1905–1954

Player with the
Most Career RBIs

Hank Aaron

Right-handed Hank Aaron batted in an incredible 2,297 runs during his 23 years in the major leagues. Aaron began his professional career with the Indianapolis Clowns, a team in the Negro American League, in 1952. He was traded to the Atlanta Braves in 1956 and won the National League batting championship with an average of .328. He was named the league's Most Valuable Player a year later when he led his team to a World Series victory. Aaron retired as a player in 1976 and was inducted into the Baseball Hall of Fame in 1982.

PLAYERS WITH THE
MOST CAREER RBIs

Runs batted in

2,297	2,213	2,076	1,995	1,951
Hank Aaron, 1952–1976	Babe Ruth, 1914–1935	Cap Anson, 1876–1897	Lou Gehrig, 1923–1939	Stan Musial, 1941–1963

Player with the
Most At Bats

Pete Rose

With 14,053 at bats, Pete Rose has stood behind the plate more than any other Major League player. Rose signed with the Cincinnati Reds after graduating high school in 1963 and played second base. During his impressive career, Rose set several other records including most singles in the Major Leagues (3,315), most seasons with 600 or more at bats in the major league (17), most career doubles in the National League (746), and most career runs in the National League (2,165). He was also named World Series MVP, Sports Illustrated Sportsman of the Year, and The Sporting News Man of the Year.

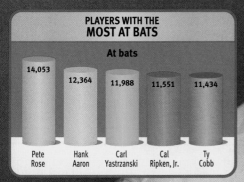

PLAYERS WITH THE MOST AT BATS

At bats

Pete Rose	Hank Aaron	Carl Yastrzanski	Cal Ripken, Jr.	Ty Cobb
14,053	12,364	11,988	11,551	11,434

Highest Career
Scoring Average

Michael Jordan

Few fans dispute the fact that Michael Jordan is basketball's greatest all-time player. During his career, he averaged an amazing 31.0 points per game. Jordan led the league in scoring for seven years. During the 1986 season, he became the second person ever to score 3,000 points in a single season. Jordan retired from playing basketball in 1998. However, from 2001 to 2003, he returned to play for the Washington Wizards.

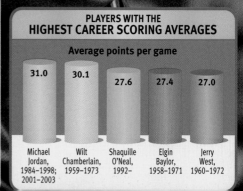

PLAYERS WITH THE HIGHEST CAREER SCORING AVERAGES

Average points per game

Michael Jordan, 1984–1998; 2001–2003	Wilt Chamberlain, 1959–1973	Shaquille O'Neal, 1992–	Elgin Baylor, 1958–1971	Jerry West, 1960–1972
31.0	30.1	27.6	27.4	27.0

Most Career
Games Played

Robert Parish

Robert Parish was a first-round draft pick by the Golden State Warriors in 1976. During his 21-year-long career, Parish played in a total of 1,611 NBA games. Parish has played in nine NBA All-Star games and was honored as one of the 50 Greatest Players in NBA History during the 1996–1997 season. He won three championships with the Boston Celtics and one with the Chicago Bulls. By the time he retired in 1997, Parish had scored an astounding 23,334 points and grabbed 14,715 rebounds.

PLAYERS WITH THE
MOST GAMES PLAYED

Games played

1,611	1,560	1,476	1,406	1,329
Robert Parish, 1976–1997	Kareem Abdul-Jabbar, 1969–1989	John Stockton, 1984–	Karl Malone, 1985–	Moses Malone, 1974–1994

WNBA Player with the
Most Career Points

Lisa Leslie

As a center for the Los Angeles Sparks, Lisa Leslie has scored 3,193 points. Leslie has a career average of 17.5 points per game. She was named MVP of the WNBA All-Star games in 1999, 2001, and 2002. Leslie was also a member of the 1996 and 2000 Olympic gold medal-winning women's basketball teams. In both 2001 and 2002, Leslie led her team to victory in the WNBA championship and was named Finals MVP. Leslie set another record on July 30, 2002, when she became the first player in WNBA history to slam dunk in a game.

**WNBA PLAYERS WITH THE
MOST CAREER POINTS**

Points scored*

Lisa Leslie, 1997–	Andrea Stinson, 1997–	Tina Thompson, 1997–	Jennifer Gillom, 1997–	Cynthia Cooper, 1997–2000
3,375	2,847	2,815	2,814	2,601

*As of June 16, 2003

WNBA Player with the Highest
Career PPG Average

Cynthia Cooper

WNBA PLAYERS WITH THE HIGHEST CAREER PPG AVERAGES

Average points per game*

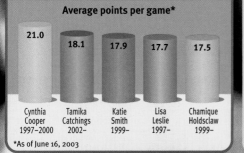

Cynthia Cooper 1997–2000	Tamika Catchings 2002–	Katie Smith 1999–	Lisa Leslie 1997–	Chamique Holdsclaw 1999–
21.0	18.1	17.9	17.7	17.5

*As of June 16, 2003

Guard Cynthia Cooper played for the Houston Comets from 1997 to 2000 and averaged 21.0 points per game (PPG). Cooper was a three-time WNBA scoring champion in 1997, 1998, and 1999, and she was the first player in the league to reach the 500, 1,000, 2,000, and 2,500 point marks. She scored 30 or more points in 16 of her 120 games and had a 92-game double-figure scoring streak from 1997 to 2000.

91

Men's Basketball Team with the Most NCAA Championships

UCLA

The University of California, Los Angeles (UCLA) has won the NCAA Basketball Championship a record 11 times. The Bruins won their 11th championship in 1995. The school has won 23 of their last 41 league titles and has been in the NCAA playoff for 35 of the last 41 years. Not surprisingly, UCLA has produced some basketball legends, too, including Kareem Abdul-Jabbar, Reggie Miller, and Baron Davis. For the last 36 years, the

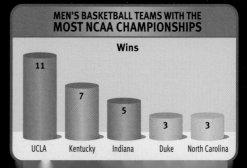

MEN'S BASKETBALL TEAMS WITH THE MOST NCAA CHAMPIONSHIPS

Wins

UCLA	Kentucky	Indiana	Duke	North Carolina
11	7	5	3	3

Women's Basketball Team with the Most NCAA Championships

Tennessee

The Tennessee Lady Volunters, or Lady Vols as they are known, have won six NCAA basketball championships. Their latest win occurred in 1998, when the Lady Vols had a perfect record of 39–0, which was the most seasonal wins ever in women's collegiate basketball. In 2003, Tennessee was in the championship but was beaten by the University of Connecticut Huskies. Since 1976, an impressive 14 Lady Vols have been to the Olympics. And, five Lady Vols have been inducted into the Women's Basketball Hall of Fame in Knoxville, Tennessee.

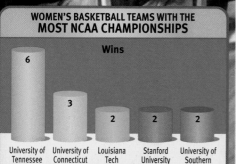

WOMEN'S BASKETBALL TEAMS WITH THE MOST NCAA CHAMPIONSHIPS

Wins

6	3	2	2	2
University of Tennessee	University of Connecticut	Louisiana Tech	Stanford University	University of Southern California

93

Player with the
Most MVP Awards

Kareem Abdul-Jabbar

Considered by most people to be one of the greatest players ever to play basketball, Kareem Abdul-Jabbar has earned six Most Valuable Player Awards. He was also an NBA Finals MVP twice. Abdul-Jabbar, a 7-foot-tall (2.1 m) center, scored double figures in an amazing 787 straight games. During his twenty-year career, this basketball legend played 1,560 games, averaging 24.6 points and 11.2 rebounds a game. He holds many impressive records, including the most blocked shots.

PLAYERS WITH THE
MOST MVP AWARDS

MVP awards

Kareem Abdul-Jabbar, 1969–1989	Michael Jordan, 1984–1998, 2001–2003	Bill Russell, 1955–1969	Larry Bird, 1979–1992	Moses Malone, 1974–1994
6	5	4	3	3

NBA's
Largest Arena

The Palace of Auburn Hills

The Palace of Auburn Hills in Michigan can seat an incredible 22,076 people for a Detroit Pistons game. The arena was built in 1988 at a cost of $70 million. It has been awarded "Arena of the Year" by *Performance* magazine seven times. Because of its excellent reputation, The Palace of Auburn Hills has been chosen to host first and second round games during the 2006 NCAA Men's Basketball Championship. It is also home to the Detroit Shock, a WNBA basketball team.

THE NBA'S LARGEST ARENAS

Seating capacity

The Palace of Auburn Hills, Michigan	United Center, Illinois	MCI Center, Washington, DC	Gund Arena, Ohio	Alamodrome, Texas
22,076	21,711	20,674	20,562	20,557

95

Most Career
Points

Kareem Abdul-Jabbar

Kareem Abdul-Jabbar scored a total of 38,387 points during his highly successful career. In 1969, Abdul-Jabbar began his NBA tenure with the Milwaukee Bucks. He was named Rookie of the Year in 1970. The following year he scored 2,596 points and helped the Bucks win the NBA championship. He was traded to the Los Angeles Lakers in 1975. With his new team, Abdul-Jabbar won the NBA championship in 1980, 1982, 1985, 1987, and 1988. He retired from basketball in 1989 and was inducted into the Basketball Hall of Fame in 1995.

PLAYERS WITH THE
MOST CAREER POINTS

Points scored

Player	Points
Kareem Abdul-Jabbar, 1969–1989	38,387
Karl Malone, 1985–	35,675
Michael Jordan, 1984–1998; 2001–2003	31,575
Wilt Chamberlain, 1959–1973	31,419
Moses Malone, 1974–1994	27,409

Country with the Most
Tour de France Wins

France

**COUNTRIES WITH THE
MOST TOUR DE FRANCE WINS**

Wins

36	18	9	8	7
France	Belgium	Italy	Spain	United States

French cyclists have won the prestigious Tour de France a record 36 times. This is not surprising because competitive cycling is a very popular pastime in the country. Two of France's most successful riders—Jacques Anquetil and Bernard Hinault—have each won the race five times. Held each July, the Tour de France lasts from 25 to 30 days. Approximately 150 cyclists compete in teams and race through about 2,000 miles (3,220 km) of France's landscape. Occasionally, the course may also extend through parts of Belgium, Spain, Germany, and Switzerland.

Bernard Hinault

Most Victories in the Indianapolis 500

A.J. Foyt, Jr., Rick Mears, and Al Unser

Al Unser

Three of professional car racing's greatest drivers—Rick Mears, A.J. Foyt, Jr., and Al Unser—have each won the Indianapolis 500 a total of four times. Of the three champion drivers, Rick Mears had the fastest time with 2 hours, 50 minutes, and 1 second in 1991. Amazingly, one of Mears's Indy 500 victories was only his second Indy race. The Indianapolis 500 is held on the Indianapolis Motor Speedway. This 2.5-mile-long (4 km) oval track has four turns. The Indy 500 is still considered the most prestigious event in all of professional racing. The race has been held each year since 1911, with the exception of World War I (1917–1918) and World War II (1942–1945).

DRIVERS WHO HAVE THE MOST INDIANAPOLIS 500 VICTORIES

Number of Indianapolis 500 races won

A.J. Foyt, Jr., 1960–1981	Rick Mears, 1977–1994	Al Unser, 1965–1987	Johnny Rutherford, 1963–1988	Bobby Unser, 1963–1981
4	4	4	3	3

Most Wins in the Daytona 500

Richard Petty

Between 1964 and 1981, Richard Petty won seven Daytona 500 races. He was the first race car driver ever to win the Daytona 500 twice. During his entire 34-year career, he won a total of 200 NASCAR races, including seven Winston Cup championships. Petty was also the first stock-car driver with winnings exceeding $1 million. By the end of his impressive career he had 356 top-5 finishes and was the first driver ever to win 10 consecutive races. His earnings totaled more than $7.7 million. Petty retired from racing in 1992.

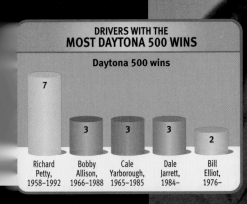

DRIVERS WITH THE MOST DAYTONA 500 WINS

Daytona 500 wins

7	3	3	3	2
Richard Petty, 1958–1992	Bobby Allison, 1966–1988	Cale Yarborough, 1965–1985	Dale Jarrett, 1984–	Bill Elliot, 1976–

Top Male World-Champion Figure Skaters

Kurt Browning, Scott Hamilton, Hayes Jenkins, and Alexei Yagudin each won 4 world championship competitions. Yagudin is from Russia and won his World Championship titles in 1998, 2000, 2001, and 2002. In the 2001–2002 season, Yagudin became the first male skater to win a gold medal in the four major skating events—Europeans, Grand Prix Final, Worlds, and the Olympics—in the same year. Browning is from Canada and was inducted into the Canadian Sports Hall of Fame in 1994. Hamilton and Jenkins are from the United States. Hamilton won the competitions from 1981 to 1984. He also won a gold medal in the 1984 Olympics. Jenkins's impressive skating career included winning every major championship between 1953 and 1956.

Kurt Browning, Scott Hamilton, Hayes Jenkins, and Alexei Yagudin

Alexei Yagudin

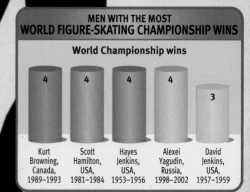

MEN WITH THE MOST WORLD FIGURE-SKATING CHAMPIONSHIP WINS

World Championship wins

Kurt Browning, Canada, 1989–1993	Scott Hamilton, USA, 1981–1984	Hayes Jenkins, USA, 1953–1956	Alexei Yagudin, Russia, 1998–2002	David Jenkins, USA, 1957–1959
4	4	4	4	3

Top Female World-Champion
Figure Skater

Carol Heiss

American figure skater Carol Heiss won the Woman's World Figure Skating championships five times between 1956 and 1960. She also won an Olympic silver medal for women's figure skating in 1956, and then a gold medal during the 1960 Winter Olympics in Squaw Valley, California. Heiss married fellow Olympic skater Hayes Jenkins (who holds a comparable record for most male world championships) and turned professional in 1961. She has been inducted into the International Women's Sports Hall of Fame and continues to coach ice skating in Ohio.

WOMEN WITH THE MOST
WORLD FIGURE-SKATING CHAMPIONSHIP WINS

World Championship wins

Carol Heiss, USA 1956–1960	Michelle Kwan, USA, 1996–2001	Katarina Witt, E. Germany, 1984–1988	Sjoukje Dijkstra, Netherlands, 1962–1964	Peggy Fleming, USA, 1966–1968
5	4	4	3	3

World's Top-Earning Male Tennis Player

Pete Sampras

During his 13 years as a professional tennis player, Pete Sampras has earned more than $43 million. That averages out to about $9,060 a day! In addition to being the top-earning male tennis player of all time, Sampras also holds several other titles. He has been named ATP Player of the Year a record six times, he has the most career game wins with 762, and he has been ranked number one for the most weeks with 276. And in 1997, Sampras became the only tennis player to be named U.S. Olympics Committee Sportsman of the Year.

THE WORLD'S TOP-EARNING MALE TENNIS PLAYERS

Career earnings in millions of US dollars

Player	Earnings
Pete Sampras 1990–	$43.3 M
Andre Agassi 1986–	$26.3 M
Boris Becker 1984–1997	$25.1 M
Yevgeny Kafelnikov 1992–	$23.2 M
Ivan Lendl 1978–1994	$21.3 M

World's Top-Earning
Female Tennis Player

Steffi Graf

During her 17-year career, Steffi Graf earned $21.8 million. After turning professional at age thirteen, Graf scored 902 victories, including 22 Grand Slam singles titles and 107 tournament titles. During her career, she was ranked number one for 377 weeks and named the WTA Player of the Year seven times. Graf's most successful year in tennis came in 1988 when she won 96% of her matches, all four Grand Slam singles titles, and an Olympic gold medal. Graf retired in 1999 and is married to tennis superstar Andre Agassi.

THE WORLD'S TOP-EARNING FEMALE TENNIS PLAYERS

Career earnings in millions of US dollars

Steffi Graf 1982–1999	Martina Navratilova 1975–1994	Martina Hingis 1994–2003	Lindsey Davenport 1993–	Monica Seles 1989–
$21.8 M	$20.5 M	$18.3 M	$14.8 M	$14.6 M

Man with the Most Singles Grand Slam Titles

Pete Sampras

Pete Sampras holds the title for the most Grand Slam male singles titles with 14 victories. He has won two Australian Opens, seven Wimbledon titles, and five U.S. Opens between 1990 and 2002. After not winning a major title in two years, Sampras was a surprise victory at the 2002 U.S. Open. He was the number 17 seed and beat Andre Agassi in a three-hour final match.

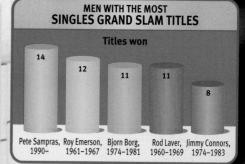

MEN WITH THE MOST SINGLES GRAND SLAM TITLES

Titles won

Pete Sampras, 1990–	Roy Emerson, 1961–1967	Bjorn Borg, 1974–1981	Rod Laver, 1960–1969	Jimmy Connors, 1974–1983
14	12	11	11	8

Woman with the Most Singles
Grand Slam Titles

**WOMEN WITH THE MOST
SINGLES GRAND SLAM TITLES**

Titles won

Margaret Court Smith, 1960–1975	Steffi Graff, 1987–1999	Helen Wills-Moody, 1923–1938	Chris Evert-Lloyd, 1974–1986	Martina Navratilova, 1974–1995
24	22	19	18	18

Between 1960 and 1975, Margaret Court Smith won 24 Grand Slam singles titles. She is the only woman ever to win the French, British, U.S., and Australian titles during one year in both the singles and doubles competitions. She was only the second woman to win all four titles in the same year. During her amazing career, she won a total of 66 Grand Slam championships—more than any other woman. Court was the world's top-seeded female player from 1962 to 1965, 1969 to 1970, and 1973. She was inducted into the International Tennis Hall of Fame in 1979.

Margaret Court Smith

Man with the Most Major Tournament Wins

Jack Nicklaus

Jack Nicklaus has won a total of 18 major championships including 6 Masters, 5 PGAs, 4 U.S. Opens, and 3 British Opens. Nicklaus was named PGA Player of the Year five times. He was a member of the winning U.S. Ryder Cup team six times, and was an individual World Cup winner a record three times. He was inducted into the World Golf Hall of Fame in 1974, just 12 years after he turned professional. He joined the U.S. Senior PGA Tour in 1990.

In addition to playing the game, Nicklaus has designed close to 200 golf courses and written a number

MEN WITH THE MOST MAJOR TOURNAMENT WINS

Major tournaments won

Jack Nicklaus, 1963–1986	Walter Hagen, 1914–1929	Ben Hogan, 1946–1953	Gary Player, 1959–1978	Tiger Woods, 1997–2002
18	11	9	9	8

LPGA Golfer with the Lowest
Seasonal Average

Annika Sorenstam

Swedish golfer Annika Sorenstam has the lowest seasonal average in the LPGA with 68.70. Sorenstam began her professional career in 1994 and has set or tied 30 LPGA records since then. In 2002, she became the first female player to finish below 69.0 with an average of 68.7. Sorenstam is currently tied for eighth place on the LGPA's career victory list. In 2003, Sorenstam became the first woman in 58 years to compete in a PGA event when she played in the Bank of America Colonial tournament.

LPGA GOLFERS WITH THE LOWEST SEASONAL AVERAGES

Seasonal average

Annika Sorenstam, 1994–	Se Ri Pak, 1998–	Karrie Webb, 1996–	Rosie Jones, 1982–	Grace Park, 2000–
68.70	69.85	70.33	70.76	70.99

Country with the Most
World Cup Points

Brazil

COUNTRIES WITH THE
MOST WORLD CUP POINTS

Total points

30	29	21	14	10
Brazil, 1958–2002	Germany/ W. Germany, 1954–2002	Italy, 1934–1982	Argentina, 1978–1986	Uruguay, 1930–1950

Brazil has accumulated 30 points in World Cup championships. (A win is worth four points, runner-up is worth three points, third place is worth two points, and fourth place is worth one point.) In Brazil, soccer is both the national sport and the national pastime. Many Brazilian superstar players are even considered national heroes. The World Cup was organized by the Federation Internationale de Football Association (FIFA) and is played every four years. This international competition was first played in 1930. Both professional and amateur players are allowed to compete.

Man with the Most
World Cup Goals

Gerd Müller

Müller Str.

Gerd Müller, a striker for West Germany, scored a total of 14 goals in the 1970 and 1974 World Cups. During his impressive soccer career, Müller competed in many other international championships and earned several awards. Müller received the Golden Boot Award (European Top Scorer) in 1970 and 1972, and the European Footballer of the Year Award in 1970. In 1970, he was also the European Championship Top Scorer and was later part of the winning European Championship team in 1972.

MEN WITH THE
MOST WORLD CUP GOALS

Goals scored

Gerd Müller, W. Germany	Just Fontaine, France	Pelé, Brazil	Ronaldo, Brazil	Sandor Kocsis, Hungary
14	13	12	12	11

Woman with the
Most CAPS

Kristine Lilly

Kristine Lilly holds the world record for the most CAPS, or international games played, with 250. This is the highest number of CAPS in both the men's and women's international soccer organizations. In world standings, she is third in all-time goals scored with 81. When she is not competing with the National Team, Lilly is a midfielder for the Boston Breakers.

WOMEN WITH THE MOST CAPS

Career CAPS

Kristine Lilly	Mia Hamm	Julie Foudy	Joy Fawcett	Tiffeny Milbrett
250	234	226	212	187
USA	USA	USA	USA	USA
1987–	1987–	1988–	1987–	1991–

Athlete with the Highest
High Jump

Charles Austin

At the 1996 Summer Games in Atlanta, Georgia, 6-foot-tall (2 m) Charles Austin sailed over a pole set at 2.3 meters (8 ft) above the ground to win a gold medal and a place in the record books. That same year, Austin was ranked number one in the world and also placed first at the Olympic Trials. This three-time Olympian has won the the U.S. Outdoor Championship six times, and the World Championship, the Indoor World Championship, and the World Cup Championship one time each.

ATHLETES WITH THE
HIGHEST OLYMPIC HIGH JUMPS

Height of jump in meters/feet

2.39 m. 7' 10"	2.38 m. 7' 9"	2.36 m. 7' 8"	2.35 m. 7' 8"	2.35 m. 7' 8"
Charles Austin USA, 1996	Hennedy Avdeyenko USSR, 1988	Gerd Wessing E. Germany, 1980	Sergey Kliugin Russia, 2000	Dietmar Mogenburg, W. Germany 1984

Athlete with the Longest
Long Jump

Bob Beamon

ATHLETES WITH THE
LONGEST OLYMPIC LONG JUMPS

Distance in meters/feet

Bob Beamon, USA, 1968	Carl Lewis, USA, 1988	Carl Lewis, USA, 1992	Ivan Pedroso, Cuba, 2000	Lutz Dombrowski, E. Germany, 1980
8.90 m. 29' 2"	8.72 m. 28' 7.5"	8.67 m. 28' 5"	8.55 m. 28'	8.54 m. 28'

After taking nineteen long strides down the runway, Bob Beamon jumped more than 29 feet (8.9 m) in length at the 1968 Olympics in Mexico City. That's almost the equivalent of jumping the length of an entire school bus! His jump broke the previous record by more than 21 inches (53 cm), and he became the first man to jump past 28 feet (8.5 m). Amazingly, twenty-two–year-old Beamon almost missed the competition because he committed two fouls in qualifying runs the day before. Beamon was elected into the Olympic Hall of Fame in 1983.

Countries with the Most Soccer Gold Medals

Hungary/ Great Britain

Both Great Britain and Hungary have each won Olympic gold medals in men's soccer a record three times. Hungary won the competition in 1952, 1964, and 1968. Great Britain triumphed in the 1900, 1908, and 1912 Olympics. In 1920, Great Britain pulled out of the competition to protest professional athletes competing in Olympic soccer, but the country rejoined in 1946. Since then, European teams have dominated the competition, and soccer remains the most popular sport throughout Europe. Soccer was first included in the 1900 and 1904 games on a trial basis, but official Olympic soccer competition began in 1908.

COUNTRIES WITH THE MOST GOLD MEDALS IN MEN'S SOCCER

Gold medals won

Great Britain	Hungary	USSR	Uruguay
3	3	2	2

Hungarian soccer player (left) and Israeli soccer player in competition

113

Most Men's Gold Medals in Swimming

Mark Spitz

U.S. swimmer Mark Spitz won nine gold medals during the 1968 Olympic Games in Mexico City and 1972 Olympics in Munich, Germany. He was also the first athlete to win seven medals during one Olympics. In his first Olympics, Spitz boasted that he would win six medals, but only took home two. But four years later, Spitz not only won all four of the individual competitions he entered, he also set world records in each. That same year, he picked up three other golds as a member of several men's relay teams.

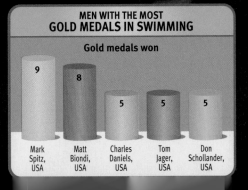

MEN WITH THE MOST GOLD MEDALS IN SWIMMING

Gold medals won

Mark Spitz, USA	Matt Biondi, USA	Charles Daniels, USA	Tom Jager, USA	Don Schollander, USA
9	8	5	5	5

Most Women's Gold Medals in Swimming

Jenny Thompson

At the 2000 Olympic Games, Jenny Thompson swam her way into the record books when she won three gold medals in Sydney, Australia. Thompson already had five gold medals from the 1992 and 1996 games. Thompson is the only U.S. woman to win eight career gold medals. She is also one of only two women to ever win three gold medals in the same event. She has won three gold medals each in the 4 x 100 free and 4 X 100 medley relay events. She has earned all of her gold medals in relay events, but has a silver and a bronze from individual competitions. During her swimming career, which began at age 8, Thompson has won 23 national titles and 26 NCAA championships.

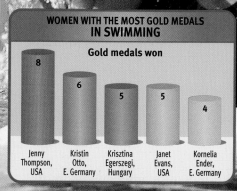

WOMEN WITH THE MOST GOLD MEDALS IN SWIMMING

Gold medals won

Jenny Thompson, USA	Kristin Otto, E. Germany	Krisztina Egerszegi, Hungary	Janet Evans, USA	Kornelia Ender, E. Germany
8	6	5	5	4

115

Most Gold Medals in Men's Track and Field

Carl Lewis/ Paavo Nurmi

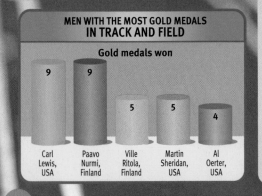

MEN WITH THE MOST GOLD MEDALS IN TRACK AND FIELD

Gold medals won

9	9	5	5	4
Carl Lewis, USA	Paavo Nurmi, Finland	Ville Ritola, Finland	Martin Sheridan, USA	Al Oerter, USA

Both Carl Lewis and Paavo Nurmi have won nine track-and-field gold medals. Paavo Nurmi set many Olympic records in his career, including the fastest 1,500 and 5,000 meter dash. He also held the record for the farthest distance run in an hour—11 miles, 1,648 yards (19,210 m). Lewis had the most wins in consecutive Olympics. Lewis won his first four gold medals in 1984 at the Los Angeles games. He later won two medals in Seoul, Korea; two more gold medals in Barcelona, Spain; and one medal in Atlanta, Georgia.

Carl Lewis

116

Most Gold Medals in Women's Track and Field

Evelyn Ashford, Fanny Blankers-Koen, Betty Cuthbert, and Bärbel Eckert Wockel

Only four women have won four gold medals in various track-and-field events. Betty Cuthbert—an Australian sprinter— won three of her medals during the 1956 Summer Olympics in Melbourne, Australia, and one at the Olympics in Tokyo. In 1984, American sprinter Evelyn Ashford became the oldest woman to win an Olympic gold in track and field. In 1948, Fanny Blankers-Koen became the first woman to win four gold medals at one Olympics. Bärbel Eckert Wockel ran in the 200-meter dash and relay races in the 1976 and 1980 Olympics.

WOMEN WITH THE MOST GOLD MEDALS IN TRACK AND FIELD

Gold medals won

Evelyn Ashford, USA	Fanny Blankers-Koen, Netherlands	Betty Cuthbert, Australia	Bärbel Eckert Wockel, E. Germany
4	4	4	4

Evelyn Ashford

Most Gold Medals in
Men's Gymnastics

Kato Sawao

During competition from 1968 to 1976, Japanese gymnast Kato Sawao won eight Olympic gold medals. He picked up his first three golds in Mexico City during the 1968 summer games, where he won for combined exercises, floor exercises, and team competition. Four years later, in Munich, Germany, Sawao won the gold in the parallel bars, and again in the combined exercises and team competition. Sawao earned his last two gold medals in Montreal, Canada, for his second consecutive win on the parallel bars and the Japanese team's fifth consecutive overall win.

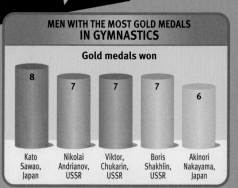

MEN WITH THE MOST GOLD MEDALS IN GYMNASTICS

Gold medals won

Kato Sawao, Japan	Nikolai Andrianov, USSR	Viktor, Chukarin, USSR	Boris Shakhlin, USSR	Akinori Nakayama, Japan
8	7	7	7	6

Most Gold Medals in
Women's Gymnastics

Larissa Latynina

Larissa Latynina won nine gold medals during her Olympic career—the first woman ever to accomplish this. A gymnast from the Soviet Union, Latynina earned her first three individual medals during the 1956 Olympic Games in Melbourne, Australia. She won the combined exercises, the vault, and the floor exercises. Four years later, in Rome, Italy, Latynina picked up her next two individual golds with repeat wins in the combined and floor exercises. She later won the gold medal for floor exercises in Tokyo, Japan, in 1964. Latynina also won a gold medal with the Soviet gymnastic team in each of her three Olympics.

**WOMEN WITH THE MOST GOLD MEDALS
IN GYMNASTICS**

Gold medals won

9	7	5	5	5
Larissa Latynina, USSR	Vera Caslavska, Czechoslovakia	Polina Astakhova, USSR	Nadia Comaneci, Romania	Agnes Keleti, Hungary

Man with the Most Figure-Skating
Gold Medals

Gillis Grafstrom

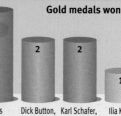

**MEN WITH THE MOST GOLD MEDALS
IN FIGURE SKATING**

Gold medals won

Gillis Grafstrom, Sweden 1920–1928	Dick Button, USA, 1948–1952	Karl Schafer, Austria, 1932–1936	Ilia Kulik, Russia, 1998	Alexei Yagudin, Russia, 2002
3	2	2	1	1

During his impressive career, Gillis Grafstrom—an artistic figure skater from Sweden—won three Olympic gold medals and one silver medal. He also won the Men's World Figure Skating Championship title a total of three times. Grafstrom developed several daring and innovative moves during his career, including the flying sit-spin. Later in his career, he coached Norwegian skater Sonja Henie to three Olympic gold medals, which propelled her into the international spotlight as a major star in world ice-skating.

Woman with the Most Figure-Skating Gold Medals

Sonja Henie

Sonja Henie won three gold medals during the Winter Olympic Games of 1928, 1932, and 1936. She won her first medal at just 15 years of age. After turning professional in 1936, she became the star of the Hollywood Ice Revues, which toured throughout America and Europe. Classical ballet training allowed Henie to create artistic routines that were very popular with the audiences. Henie was also a popular actress who made 10 motion pictures. When she passed away in 1969, she was one of the wealthiest women in the world.

WOMEN WITH THE MOST GOLD MEDALS IN FIGURE SKATING

Gold medals won

Skater	Gold medals won
Sonja Henie, Norway, 1928–1936	3
Katarina Witt, E. Germany, 1984–1988	2
Oksana Baiul, Ukraine, 1994	1
Sarah Hughes, USA, 2002	1
Tara Lipinski, USA, 1998	1

World's Fastest
Bobsled Time

Germany II

THE WORLD'S
FASTEST BOBSLED TIMES

2:39.41	3:07.51	3:20.22	3:27.28	3:40.43
Germany II 1998	Germany II 2002	East Germany 1984	Germany 1994	East Germany 1976

At the 1998 Winter Olympics in Nagano, Japan, Germany II sped down the bobsled track and into the history books with a record-breaking time of 2:39.41. The team of four men—Christoph Langen, Markus Zimmermann, Marco Jakobs, and Olaf Hampel—followed the German tradition of excellence in bobsledding. In fact, the five fastest bobsled times were all accomplished by Germans. A bobsled can reach a speed of 90 miles (145 km) per hour, and the crew feels five times the force of gravity when braking. The sport became an Olympic competition in 1924.

Country with the
Most Medals

United States

Since the time that the United States competed in the first modern Olympics in 1896, it has won a total of 2,341 medals—950 gold, 743 silver, and 648 bronze. In some sports, most notably basketball and the long jump, the United States has dominated the field, often winning the gold year after year. The United States has hosted the games eight times— four Winter Games and four Summer Games. During some competitions, like the 1980 Olympic Games held in Moscow, U.S.S.R., the United States chose not to compete for political reasons.

COUNTRIES WITH THE
MOST OLYMPIC MEDALS

Medals won

USA	USSR	Great Britain	France	Sweden
2,341	1,324	654	620	479

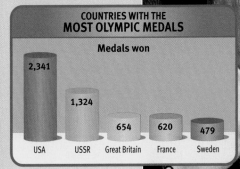

Skeleton gold medalist Jimmy Shea

123

Top Career
Gold Medal Winners

Larissa Latynina, Carl Lewis, Paavo Nurmi, Mark Spitz

Mark Spitz

During their Olympic careers, Larissa Latynina, Carl Lewis, Paavo Nurmi, and Mark Spitz each won nine gold medals. Lewis, an American sprinter and jumper, won his medals between 1984 and 1996. Gymnast Latynina, the only woman to win nine medals, competed during the 1950s and 1960s. Nurmi, a track-and-field athlete from Finland, won his nine medals between 1920 and 1928. American Spitz won his medals in swimming competitions between 1968 and 1972.

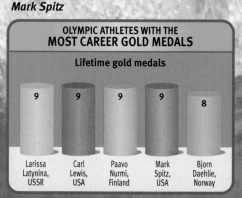

**OLYMPIC ATHLETES WITH THE
MOST CAREER GOLD MEDALS**

Lifetime gold medals

Larissa Latynina, USSR	Carl Lewis, USA	Paavo Nurmi, Finland	Mark Spitz, USA	Bjorn Daehlie, Norway
9	9	9	9	8

Olympics with the
Most Competitors

Sydney, Australia 2000

In September 2000, some 10,651 competitors traveled to Sydney, Australia, to take part in the largest Olympics ever. A crowd of 110,000 spectators cheered the athletes at the opening ceremonies. The athletes stayed in an Olympic Village that featured a gym, café, video arcade, and night club. The United States, which sent 600 competitors, won the most medals with 97, followed by the Russian Federation (88) and China (59). More than a million spectators and athletes gathered for the closing ceremonies at Stadium Australia. The Games concluded with a spectacular fireworks display over the Harbour Bridge.

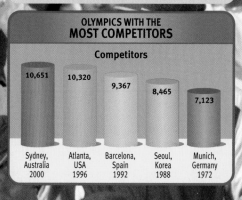

**OLYMPICS WITH THE
MOST COMPETITORS**

Competitors

Sydney, Australia 2000	Atlanta, USA 1996	Barcelona, Spain 1992	Seoul, Korea 1988	Munich, Germany 1972
10,651	10,320	9,367	8,465	7,123

Canadian athletes at the 2000 Summer Olympics

Most Career Points

Wayne Gretzky

During his 20-year career, Wayne Gretzky scored an unbelievable 2,857 points and 894 goals. In fact, Gretzky was the first person in the NHL to average more than two points per game. Many people consider Canadian-born Gretzky to be the greatest player in the history of the National Hockey League. In fact, he is called the "Great One." He officially retired from the sport in 1999 and was inducted into the Hockey Hall of Fame that same year. After his final game, the NHL retired his jersey number (99).

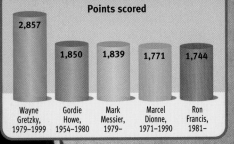

PLAYERS WHO SCORED THE MOST CAREER POINTS

Points scored

Wayne Gretzky, 1979–1999	Gordie Howe, 1954–1980	Mark Messier, 1979–	Marcel Dionne, 1971–1990	Ron Francis, 1981–
2,857	1,850	1,839	1,771	1,744

Team with the Most
Stanley Cup Wins

Montreal Canadiens

Between 1916 and 1993, the Montreal Canadiens have won an amazing 24 Stanley Cup victories. That's almost one-quarter of all the Stanley Cups ever played. The team plays at Montreal's Molson Center. The Canadiens were created in December 1909 by J. Ambrose O'Brien to play for the National Hockey Association (NHA). They eventually made the transition into the National Hockey League. Over the years, the Canadiens have included such great players as Maurice Richard, George Hainsworth, Jacques Lemaire, Saku Koivu, and Emile Bouchard.

TEAMS WITH THE MOST
STANLEY CUP WINS

Stanley Cups won

24	11	10	5	5
Montreal Canadiens, 1916–1993	Toronto Maple Leafs, 1932–1967	Detroit Red Wings, 1936–2002	Boston Bruins, 1929–1972	Edmonton Oilers, 1984–1990

Montreal Canadiens with Stanley Cup

Most Points in a Single Game

Darryl Sittler

PLAYERS WITH THE MOST
POINTS EARNED IN A SINGLE GAME

Points

Darryl Sittler, 1976	Tom Bladon, 1977	Bert Olmstead, 1954	Maurice Richard, 1944	Bryan Trotier, 1978
10	8	8	8	8

Toronto Maple Leaf Darryl Sittler scored 6 goals and had 4 assists to earn a record total of 10 points in a game against the Boston Bruins on February 7, 1976. In an added dramatic flourish, the last goal he scored was actually from behind the net. Sittler tried to pass to a teammate, but the puck bounced off another player's leg and into the net instead. Sittler played professionally for 15 seasons in the National Hockey League and was inducted into the Hockey Hall of Fame in 1989.

Goalie with the
Most Career Wins

Patrick Roy

Patrick Roy won 551 games during his impressive hockey career. Roy also holds the NHL records for most 30-or-more win seasons (11), most playoff games played (240), most playoff minutes played (14,783), and most playoff wins (148). He was also a member of the Montreal Canadiens when they won the Stanley Cup in 1986 and 1993. Roy helped his team—the Colorado Avalanche—to win the Stanley Cup Championships in 1996 and 2001. On May 29, 2003, Roy announced his retirement from the sport.

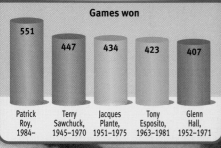

GOALTENDERS WITH THE
MOST CAREER WINS

Games won

Patrick Roy, 1984–	Terry Sawchuck, 1945–1970	Jacques Plante, 1951–1975	Tony Esposito, 1963–1981	Glenn Hall, 1952–1971
551	447	434	423	407

Nature Records

Animals • Disasters • Food
Natural Formations • Plants • Weather

World's Sleepiest Animal

Koala

A koala will spend the majority of its day—about 22 hours—sleeping in its eucalyptus tree. Its sharp claws and nimble feet help it to hold on to the branches, even when it is asleep. Koalas are nocturnal animals, which means they are active mainly at night. During the 2 hours a koala is awake, it will feed on 1 to 2 pounds (.4 to .9 kg) of eucalyptus leaves. When a koala is born, it measures about 3/4 inch (1.9 cm) long and lives in its mother's pouch for six months. An average koala is about 2 feet (.6 m) tall and weighs about 22 pounds (10 kg).

THE WORLD'S SLEEPIEST ANIMALS

Hours of sleep per day

Koala	Sloth	Armadillo	Opossum	Lemur
22	20	19	19	16

World's
Fastest Land Mammal

Cheetah

These sleek mammals can reach a speed of 65 miles (105 km) per hour for short spurts. Their quickness enables these large African cats to easily outrun their prey. All other African cats must stalk their prey because they lack the cheetah's amazing speed. Unlike the paws of all other cats, cheetah paws do not have skin sheaths—thin protective coverings. Their claws, therefore, cannot pull back.

THE WORLD'S
FASTEST LAND MAMMALS

Maximum speed in miles/kilometers per hour

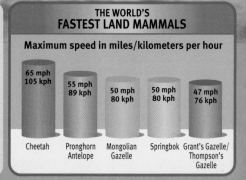

65 mph 105 kph	55 mph 89 kph	50 mph 80 kph	50 mph 80 kph	47 mph 76 kph
Cheetah	Pronghorn Antelope	Mongolian Gazelle	Springbok	Grant's Gazelle/ Thompson's Gazelle

World's
Slowest Land Mammal

Sloth

When a three-toed sloth is traveling on the ground, it reaches a top speed of only .07 miles (.11 km) per hour. That means that it would take the animal almost 15 minutes to cross a four-lane street. The main reason sloths move so slowly is that they cannot walk like other mammals. They must pull themselves along the ground using only their sharp claws. Because of this, sloths spend the majority of their time in trees. A green algae grows on their fur, camouflaging them in the trees. Surprisingly, sloths are distantly related to armadillos and anteaters.

SOME OF THE WORLD'S
SLOWEST ANIMALS

Maximum speed in miles/kilometers per hour

Sloth	Spider	Chicken	Pig	Squirrel
.07 mph .11 kph	1.2 mph 1.9 kph	9 mph 14 kph	11 mph 18 kph	12 mph 19 kph

133

World's
Smallest Mammal

Kitti's Hog-nosed Bat

THE WORLD'S SMALLEST MAMMALS

Length in inches/centimeters

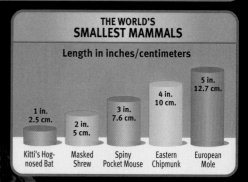

Kitti's Hog-nosed Bat	Masked Shrew	Spiny Pocket Mouse	Eastern Chipmunk	European Mole
1 in. 2.5 cm.	2 in. 5 cm.	3 in. 7.6 cm.	4 in. 10 cm.	5 in. 12.7 cm.

The Kitti's hog-nosed bat weighs a mere .25 ounce (7.1 g) and measures about 1 inch (2.5 cm) wide. This means that the world's smallest mammal is actually the size of a bumblebee. Even when its wings are extended, this member of the bat family measures only 6 inches (15 cm) wide. This tiny creature is found only in Thailand. It lives in the limestone caves near the Kwae Noi River. Like most bats, Kitti's hog-nosed bats are most active from dusk until dawn and feed mostly on insects.

World's Tallest
Land Mammal

Giraffe

Giraffes can grow to more than 18 feet (5.5 m) in height. That means an average giraffe could look through the window of a two-story building. A giraffe's neck is 18 times longer than a human's, but both mammals have exactly the same number of neck bones. A giraffe's long legs enable it to outrun most of its enemies. When cornered, a giraffe has been known to kill a lion with a single kick.

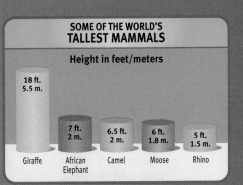

SOME OF THE WORLD'S TALLEST MAMMALS

Height in feet/meters

18 ft. 5.5 m.	7 ft. 2 m.	6.5 ft. 2 m.	6 ft. 1.8 m.	5 ft. 1.5 m.
Giraffe	African Elephant	Camel	Moose	Rhino

World's Heaviest
Marine Mammal

Blue Whale

THE WORLD'S
HEAVIEST MARINE MAMMALS

Weight in tons/metric tons

143.3 tons 130 t.	49.6 tons 45 t.	44.1 tons 40 t.	39.7 tons 36 t.	36.0 tons 33 t.
Blue Whale	Fin Whale	Right Whale	Sperm Whale	Gray Whale

Blue whales can weigh more than 143 tons (130 t) and measure over 100 feet (30 m) long, making these enormous sea creatures the largest animals that have ever lived. Amazingly, these gentle giants only eat krill—small, shrimplike animals. A blue whale can eat about 4 tons (3.6 t) of krill each day in the summer, when food is plentiful . To catch the krill, a whale gulps as much as 17,000 gallons (64,600 l) of seawater into its mouth at one time. Then it uses its tongue—which can be the same size as a car—to push the water back out. The krill get caught in hairs on the whale's baleen (a keratin structure that hangs down from the roof of the whale's mouth).

World's Heaviest
Land Mammal

African Elephant

African elephants measure approximately 24 feet (7.3 m) long and can weigh up to 6 tons (5.4 t). Even at their great size, they are strictly vegetarian. They will, however, eat up to 500 pounds (226 kg) of vegetation a day! Their two tusks—which are really elongated teeth—grow continuously during their lives and can reach about 9 feet (2.7 m) in length. These large animals move at about 4 miles (6.4 km) per hour, but they can charge at 30 miles (48 km) per hour.

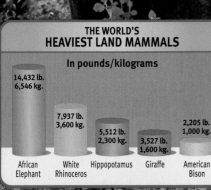

THE WORLD'S HEAVIEST LAND MAMMALS

In pounds/kilograms

African Elephant	14,432 lb. / 6,546 kg.
White Rhinoceros	7,937 lb. / 3,600 kg.
Hippopotamus	5,512 lb. / 2,300 kg.
Giraffe	3,527 lb. / 1,600 kg.
American Bison	2,205 lb. / 1,000 kg.

World's
Largest Rodent

Capybara

Also known as water hogs and carpinchos, capybaras reach an average length of 4 feet (1.2 m), stand about 20 inches (51 cm) tall, and weigh between 75 and 150 pounds (34 to 68 kg)! That's about the same size as a Labrador retriever. Capybaras are found in South and Central America, where they spend much of their time in groups looking for food. They are strictly vegetarian and have been known to raid gardens for melons and squash. Their partially webbed feet make capybaras excellent swimmers. Capybaras are hunted for food and their hides are used for gloves and clothing.

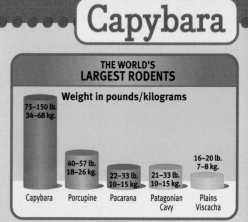

THE WORLD'S LARGEST RODENTS

Weight in pounds/kilograms

Capybara	Porcupine	Pacarana	Patagonian Cavy	Plains Viscacha
75–150 lb. 34–68 kg.	40–57 lb. 18–26 kg.	22–33 lb. 10–15 kg.	21–33 lb. 10–15 kg.	16–20 lb. 7–8 kg.

World's Longest-Lived
Mammal

Killer Whale

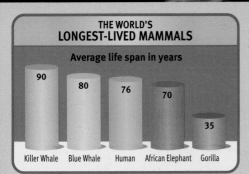

**THE WORLD'S
LONGEST-LIVED MAMMALS**

Average life span in years

Killer Whale	Blue Whale	Human	African Elephant	Gorilla
90	80	76	70	35

The average life span of a killer whale is 90 years. The average life span of a human is only about 76 years. Male killer whales can measure up to 28 feet (9m) long and weigh up to 12,000 pounds (5,443 kg). They have more than 4 dozen razor-sharp teeth and use them to feed on both birds and mammals. Some of these whales have been known to eat up to 2,000 pounds (907 kg) in just one feeding.

World's
Fastest Flyer

Peregrine Falcon

When diving through the air, a peregrine falcon can reach speeds of up to 175 miles (282 km) an hour. That's about the same speed as the fastest race car in the Indianapolis 500. These powerful birds can catch prey in midair and kill it instantly with their sharp claws. Peregrine falcons range from about 13 to 19 inches (33 to 48 cm) long. The female is called a falcon, but the male is called a tercel, which means "one-third" in German. This is because the male is about one-third the size of the female.

THE WORLD'S FASTEST FLYERS

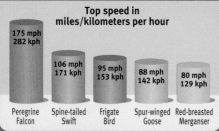

Top speed in miles/kilometers per hour

Peregrine Falcon	Spine-tailed Swift	Frigate Bird	Spur-winged Goose	Red-breasted Merganser
175 mph 282 kph	106 mph 171 kph	95 mph 153 kph	88 mph 142 kph	80 mph 129 kph

World's Largest
Bird Wingspan

Marabou Stork

The Marabou stork has the largest wingspan of any bird. With a wingspan that can reach up to 13 feet (4 m), these large storks weigh up to 20 pounds (9 kg) and can grow up to 5 feet (150 cm) tall. Their long leg and toe bones are actually hollow. This adaptation is very important for flight because it makes the bird lighter. Although marabous eat insects, small mammals, and fish, the majority of their food is carrion—already dead meat. Since these storks need to eat about 1.5 pounds (700 g) of food a day, this makes them an important part of nature's clean-up crew.

THE WORLD'S LARGEST BIRD WINGSPANS

Wingspan in feet/meters

Marabou Stork	Albatross	Trumpeter Swan	Mute Swan	Whooper Swan
13 ft. 4 m.	12 ft. 3.7 m.	11 ft. 3.4 m.	10 ft. 3 m.	10 ft. 3 m

Bird That Builds the
Largest Nest

Bald Eagle

A bald eagle's nest can measure 8 feet (2.4 m) wide and 16 feet (4.9 m) deep. These birds of prey have wingspans up to 7.5 feet (2.3m) and need a home that they can nest in comfortably. By carefully constructing their home with sticks, branches, and plant material, a pair of bald eagles can balance their home—which can weigh up to 4,000 pounds (8,800 kg)—on the top of a tree or cliff. Called an aerie, this home will be used for the rest of the eagles' lives. Each year a bald eagle pair will add on to their nest as they prepare to raise more offspring.

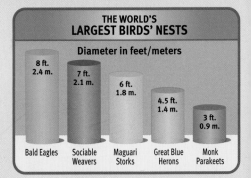

THE WORLD'S LARGEST BIRDS' NESTS

Diameter in feet/meters

8 ft. 2.4 m.	7 ft. 2.1 m.	6 ft. 1.8 m.	4.5 ft. 1.4 m.	3 ft. 0.9 m.
Bald Eagles	Sociable Weavers	Maguari Storks	Great Blue Herons	Monk Parakeets

World's Largest
Flightless Bird

Ostrich

An ostrich can grow up to 8 feet (2.4 m) tall and weigh up to 300 pounds (136 kg). Ostriches also have the largest eyeballs of the bird class, measuring 2 inches (5 cm) across. These African birds lay giant eggs, averaging 3 pounds (1.4 kg) each. Ostriches can run at speeds of up to 50 miles (80.5 km) per hour. With their long legs, they can cover 15 feet (4.6 m) in a single bound. Ostriches live on the hot, grassy plains of Africa and eat plants, insects, seeds, and fruits.

THE WORLD'S LARGEST FLIGHTLESS BIRDS

Height in inches/centimeters

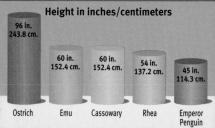

Ostrich	Emu	Cassowary	Rhea	Emperor Penguin
96 in. 243.8 cm.	60 in. 152.4 cm.	60 in. 152.4 cm.	54 in. 137.2 cm.	45 in. 114.3 cm.

World's
Smallest Bird

From the tip of its bill to the end of its tail, the male bee hummingbird measures barely 2.5 inches (6.3 cm) long. In fact, its tail and bill alone make up one-half of the bird's length, which is about equal to the width of a baseball card. Bee hummingbirds, which weigh only about .07 ounce (2 g), are also able to beat their wings at speeds of up to 80 times per second. Like most other hummingbirds, they are able to fly forward, backward, and straight up and down. They also have the unique ability to hover in midair. These tiny flying creatures are found in Cuba and on the Isle of Pines in the South Pacific.

THE WORLD'S SMALLEST BIRDS

Length in inches/centimeters

Bee Hummingbird	Pygmy Parrot	New Zealand Wren	Gouldian Finch	Least Sandpiper
2.5 in. 6.3 cm.	3.5 in. 9.0 cm.	3.5 in. 9.0 cm.	4.0 in. 10.0 cm.	4.5 in. 11.0 cm.

Bee Hummingbird

World's
Largest Bird Egg

Ostrich Egg

An ostrich egg can measure 5 inches by 6 inches (13 cm by 16 cm) long and weigh up to 4 pounds (1.8 kg). In fact, just one ostrich egg equals up to 24 chicken eggs. The egg yolk makes up one-third of the volume. Although the egg shell is only 2 mm thick, it is tough enough to withstand the weight of a 345-pound (157-kg) ostrich. A hen ostrich can lay from 10 to 70 eggs each year. Females usually are able to recognize their own eggs, even when they are mixed in with those of other females in their shared nest.

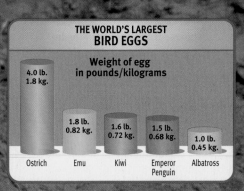

THE WORLD'S LARGEST BIRD EGGS

Weight of egg in pounds/kilograms

Ostrich	Emu	Kiwi	Emperor Penguin	Albatross
4.0 lb. 1.8 kg.	1.8 lb. 0.82 kg.	1.6 lb. 0.72 kg.	1.5 lb. 0.68 kg.	1.0 lb. 0.45 kg.

World's Fastest Flying Insect

Hawk Moth

The average hawk moth—which got its name from its swift and steady flight—can cruise along at speeds of up to 33 miles (53 km) per hour. That's faster than the average speed limit on most city streets. Although they are found throughout the world, most species live in tropical climates. Also known as the sphinx moth and the hummingbird moth, this large insect can have a wingspan that reaches up to 8 inches (20 cm). When alarmed, one species can produce loud squawking noises by blowing air through its tongue.

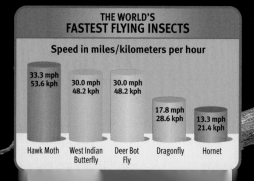

THE WORLD'S FASTEST FLYING INSECTS

Speed in miles/kilometers per hour

Hawk Moth	West Indian Butterfly	Deer Bot Fly	Dragonfly	Hornet
33.3 mph 53.6 kph	30.0 mph 48.2 kph	30.0 mph 48.2 kph	17.8 mph 28.6 kph	13.3 mph 21.4 kph

World's Longest Insect

Stick Insect

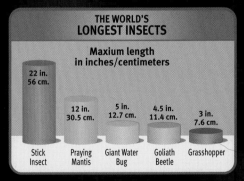

THE WORLD'S LONGEST INSECTS

Maxium length in inches/centimeters

22 in. 56 cm.	12 in. 30.5 cm.	5 in. 12.7 cm.	4.5 in. 11.4 cm.	3 in. 7.6 cm.
Stick Insect	Praying Mantis	Giant Water Bug	Goliath Beetle	Grasshopper

Measuring more than 22 inches (56 cm) in length, the tropical stick insect is almost the same size as an average television screen. All together, there are about 2,000 species of stick insects. They feed on plants and are mostly nocturnal. Most have long, thin brown or green bodies. Their twiglike appearance camouflages them well. When they are still, stick insects look just like part of a plant or tree. Their eggs are also camouflaged and look like tiny, hard seeds. All stick insects have the ability to grow back a leg or antenna that has broken off.

World's
Smallest Fish

Dwarf Pygmy Goby

The dwarf pygmy goby is the world's smallest fish, measuring only .5 inch (13 mm) long at the most. It is also one of the smallest living animals with a backbone. Unlike most gobies, this species lives in freshwater and can be found mainly in the Philippines. These fish must, however, swim to saltwater to breed and hatch their eggs. Gobies usually lay only a few eggs at a time and sometimes care briefly for their young, which are called ipon.

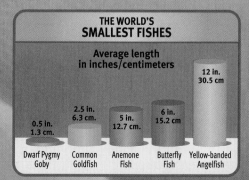

THE WORLD'S SMALLEST FISHES

Average length in inches/centimeters

Dwarf Pygmy Goby	Common Goldfish	Anemone Fish	Butterfly Fish	Yellow-banded Angelfish
0.5 in. 1.3 cm.	2.5 in. 6.3 cm.	5 in. 12.7 cm.	6 in. 15.2 cm	12 in. 30.5 cm

World's
Biggest Fish

Whale Shark

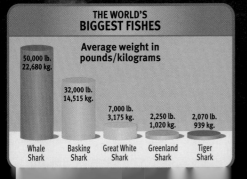

THE WORLD'S BIGGEST FISHES

Average weight in pounds/kilograms

Whale Shark	Basking Shark	Great White Shark	Greenland Shark	Tiger Shark
50,000 lb. 22,680 kg.	32,000 lb. 14,515 kg.	7,000 lb. 3,175 kg.	2,250 lb. 1,020 kg.	2,070 lb. 939 kg.

Whale sharks grow to an average of 30 feet (9 m) in length, but many have been known to reach up to 60 feet (18 m) long. That's the same length as two school buses! Whale sharks also weigh an average of 50,000 pounds (22,680 kg). As with most sharks, the females are larger than the males. Their mouths measure about 5 feet (1.5 m) long and contain about 3,000 teeth. Amazingly, these gigantic fish eat only microscopic plankton and tiny fish. They float near the surface looking for food

World's
Fastest Fish

Sailfish

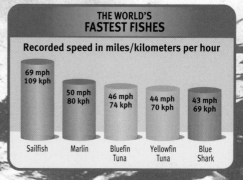

THE WORLD'S FASTEST FISHES

Recorded speed in miles/kilometers per hour

Sailfish	Marlin	Bluefin Tuna	Yellowfin Tuna	Blue Shark
69 mph 109 kph	50 mph 80 kph	46 mph 74 kph	44 mph 70 kph	43 mph 69 kph

Although it is difficult to measure the exact speed of fish, a sailfish once grabbed a fishing line and dragged it 300 feet (91 m) away in just 3 seconds. That means it was swimming at an average speed of 69 miles (109 km) per hour—just higher than the average speed limit on the highway! Sailfish are very large—they average 6 feet (1.8 m) long, but can grow up to 11 feet (3.4 m). Sailfish eat squid and surface-dwelling fish. Sometimes several sailfish will work together to catch their prey.

World's Slowest Fish

Sea Horse

Sea horses move around the ocean at just .001 miles (.002 km) per hour. At that rate of speed, it would take the fish about an hour to swim only 50 feet (15 m). Sea horses spend most of their time near the shore. There, they can hold on to plants with their tails. This helps them avoid enemies. Approximately 50 different species of sea horses are found throughout the world. However, due to over-harvesting, the sea horse population has decreased by up to 95%. Poachers catch sea horses to stock aquariums and also to use as medicines in some countries.

SOME OF THE WORLD'S SLOWEST FISHES

Average speed in miles/kilometers

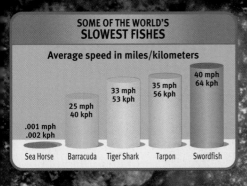

Sea Horse	Barracuda	Tiger Shark	Tarpon	Swordfish
.001 mph .002 kph	25 mph 40 kph	33 mph 53 kph	35 mph 56 kph	40 mph 64 kph

World's
Largest Mollusk

Giant Squid

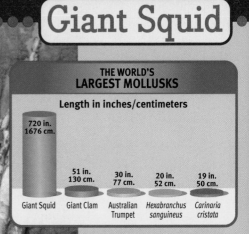

THE WORLD'S LARGEST MOLLUSKS

Length in inches/centimeters

Giant Squid	Giant Clam	Australian Trumpet	*Hexabranchus sanguineus*	*Carinaria cristata*
720 in. 1676 cm.	51 in. 130 cm.	30 in. 77 cm.	20 in. 52 cm.	19 in. 50 cm.

The giant squid measures at least 60 feet long (18 m), with tentacles as long as 40 feet (12.2 m) and eyes the size of hubcaps. This giant sea creature may have even more impressive measurements, but scientists have had a very difficult time studying this elusive creature. Living at depths of up to 1,970 feet (600 m) below sea level, scientists have only been able to study dead giant squid that have been caught in fishing nets or eaten by sperm whales. Fewer than 50 giant squid have been found in the last century. As underwater technology advances, scientists hope to be able to study this giant mollusk in greater detail.

Snake with the
Longest Fangs

Gaboon Viper

The Gaboon viper has fangs that measure 2 inches (5 cm) in length! These giant fangs fold up against the snake's mouth so it does not pierce its own skin. When it is ready to strike its prey, the fangs snap down into position. The snake can grow up to 7 feet (2 m) long and weigh 18 pounds (8 kg). It is found in Africa and is perfectly camouflaged for hunting on the ground beneath leaves and grasses. The Gaboon viper's poison is not as toxic as some other snakes, but it is quite dangerous because of the amount of poison it can inject at one time. The snake is not very aggressive, however, and usually only attacks when bothered.

SNAKES WITH THE LONGEST FANGS

Fang length in inches/centimeters

Gaboon Viper	Bushmaster	Black Mamba	Diamondback Rattlesnake	Australian Taipan
2.0 in. 5.1 cm.	1.5 in. 3.8 cm.	1.0 in. 2.5 cm.	1.0 in. 2.5 cm.	0.7 in. 1.8 cm.

World's
Deadliest Snake

Black Mamba

One African black mamba snake bite releases a venom powerful enough to kill up to 200 humans. A bite from this snake is almost always fatal if it is not treated immediately. This large member of the cobra family grows to about 14 feet (4.3 m) long. In addition to its deadly poison, it is also a very aggressive snake. It will raise its body off the ground when it feels threatened. It then spreads its hood and strikes swiftly at its prey with its long front teeth. Depending on its age, it can range in color from gray to green to black.

THE WORLD'S DEADLIEST SNAKES

Deaths possible per bite

Black Mamba	Taipan	Russell's Viper	Common Krait	Forest Cobra
200	170	150	60	50

World's Most
Deadly Amphibian

Poison Dart Frog

Poison dart frogs are found mostly in the tropical rain forests of Central and South America, where they live on the moist land. These lethal amphibians have enough poison in their skin to kill up to 20 adult humans. A dart frog's poison is so effective that native Central and South Americans sometimes coat their hunting arrows or hunting darts with it. These brightly colored frogs can be yellow, orange, red, green, blue, or any combination of these colors and measure only .5 to 2 inches (1 to 5 cm) long. They feed mostly on beetles, ants, termites, and other insects by capturing them with their sticky tongues.

SOME OF THE WORLD'S POISONOUS AMPHIBIANS

Length in inches/centimeters

Poison Dart Frog	Black and Yellow Spotted Frog	Fire-bellied Toad	European Salamander	Canetoad
2 in. 5.1 cm.	2.5 in. 6.4 cm.	3 in. 7.6 cm.	4 in. 10 cm.	10 in. 25.4 cm.

World's
Longest Snake

Reticulated Python

The average adult reticulated python is about 17 feet (5 m) long, but some can grow to more than 27 feet (8.2 m) in length. That's almost the length of an average school bus. These pythons live mostly in Asia, from Myanmar to Indonesia to the Philippines. The python has teeth that curve backward and can hold the snake's prey still. It hunts mainly at night and will eat mammals and birds. Reticulated pythons are slow-moving creatures that kill their prey by constriction, or strangulation.

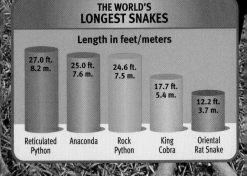

THE WORLD'S LONGEST SNAKES

Length in feet/meters

Reticulated Python	Anaconda	Rock Python	King Cobra	Oriental Rat Snake
27.0 ft. 8.2 m.	25.0 ft. 7.6 m.	24.6 ft. 7.5 m.	17.7 ft. 5.4 m.	12.2 ft. 3.7 m.

World's
Largest Lizard

Komodo Dragon

These large members of the monitor family can grow to 10 feet (3 m) in length and weigh about 300 pounds (136 kg). A Komodo dragon has a long neck and tail, and strong legs. They are found mainly on Komodo Island. Komodos are dangerous and have even been known to attack and kill humans. A Komodo uses its sense of smell to locate food. It uses its long, yellow tongue to pick up an animal's scent. A Komodo can consume 80% of its body weight in just one meal!

**THE WORLD'S
LARGEST LIZARDS**

Length in feet/meters

Komodo Dragon	Water Monitor	Perenty	Common Iguana	Marine Iguana
10.0 ft. 3.0 m.	8.8 ft. 2.7 m.	7.8 ft. 2.4 m.	5.0 ft. 1.5 m.	5.0 ft. 1.5 m.

World's Largest Reptile

Saltwater Crocodile

These enormous reptiles can measure more than 22 feet (6.7 m) long. That's about twice the length of the average car. However, males usually measure only about 17 feet (5 m) long, and females normally reach about 10 feet (3 m) in length. A large adult will feed on buffalo, monkeys, cattle, wild boar, and other large mammals. Saltwater crocodiles are found throughout the East Indies and Australia. Despite their name, saltwater crocodiles can also be found in freshwater and swamps. Some other common names for this species are estuarial crocodile and the Indo-Pacific crocodile.

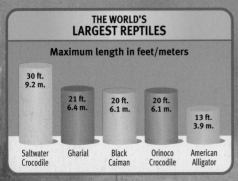

THE WORLD'S LARGEST REPTILES

Maximum length in feet/meters

30 ft. 9.2 m.	21 ft. 6.4 m.	20 ft. 6.1 m.	20 ft. 6.1 m.	13 ft. 3.9 m.
Saltwater Crocodile	Gharial	Black Caiman	Orinoco Crocodile	American Alligator

World's
Largest Amphibian

Chinese Giant Salamander

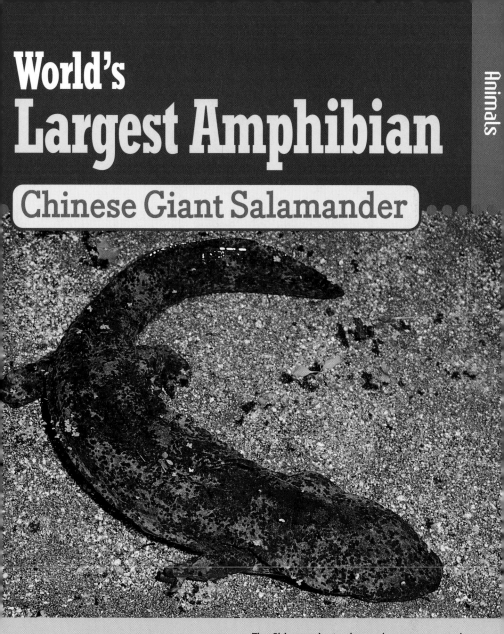

THE WORLD'S LARGEST AMPHIBIANS

Size in inches/centimeters

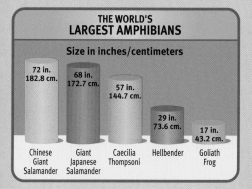

72 in. 182.8 cm.	68 in. 172.7 cm.	57 in. 144.7 cm.	29 in. 73.6 cm.	17 in. 43.2 cm.
Chinese Giant Salamander	Giant Japanese Salamander	Caecilia Thompsoni	Hellbender	Goliath Frog

The Chinese giant salamander can grow to almost 6 feet (1.8 m) in length and weigh up to 55 pounds (25 kg). This amphibian has a large head, but its eyes and nostrils are small. It has short legs, a long tail, and very smooth skin. This large amphibian can be found in the streams of northeastern, central, and southern China. It feeds on fish, frogs, crabs, and snakes. The giant Chinese salamander will not hunt its prey. It will wait until a potential meal wanders too close and then grab it in its mouth. Because many people enjoy the taste of the salamander's meat, it is often hunted and its population is shrinking.

World's Longest-Lived Reptile

Galápagos Turtle

Some of these giant reptiles have been known to live for more than 150 years. Galápagos turtles are also some of the largest turtles in the world, weighing in at up to 500 pounds (226 kg). Even at their great size, these turtles can pull their heads, tails, and legs completely inside their shells. Amazingly, Galápagos turtles can go without eating or drinking for many weeks. This is partly because it can take them up to three weeks to digest a meal!

THE WORLD'S LONGEST-LIVED REPTILES

Maximum age in years

Galápagos Turtle	Box Turtle	American Alligator	Boa Constrictor	Komodo Dragon
150	120	50	30	20

Deadliest Twentieth-Century Flood

Huang He River

THE TWENTIETH CENTURY'S DEADLIEST FLOODS

Estimated deaths

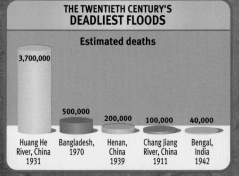

3,700,000	500,000	200,000	100,000	40,000
Huang He River, China 1931	Bangladesh, 1970	Henan, China 1939	Chang Jiang River, China 1911	Bengal, India 1942

In August 1931, the powerful floodwaters from the Huang He River in China burst through villages and towns killing an estimated 3.7 million people. It was not the first time the Huang He—also known as the Yellow River—has caused disaster. This 3,000-mile- (4,828-km) long river has flooded its surrounding areas more than 1,500 times in the last 1,800 years. It has even changed its course nine times. The Chinese have tried building dams, dikes, and overflow channels to control the river, but during the summer flood season, many of the structures collapse under the immense pressure of the surging waters.

Deadliest Twentieth-Century Earthquake

Tangshan

Tangshan, China, was rocked by a deadly earthquake on July 28, 1976. The tragedy devastated the city, killing more than 242,000 people—about one-quarter of its total population. Since that time, Tangshan has come to be known as the "Brave City of China" because of its successful rebuilding efforts. With its new earthquake-proof buildings and an impressive high-tech transportation system, the city now plays an important role in China's economy. Tangshan is a major supplier of fish, iron ore, and fruits and vegetables.

**THE TWENTIETH CENTURY'S
DEADLIEST EARTHQUAKES**

Estimated deaths

242,419	200,000	180,000	160,000	142,807
Tangshan, China 1976	Nan Shan, China 1927	Kansu, China 1927	Messina, Italy 1908	Tokyo/Yokohama, Japan 1923

Deadliest Twentieth-Century
Volcanic Eruption

Mount Pelée

Mount Pelée erupted on May 8, 1902, and killed about 30,000 people living on the small island of Martinique in the Caribbean Sea. By the time the eruption subsided, about 15% of the island's population had been killed. The most devastating part of the eruption was the tremendously hot ash flows. The flows destroyed the port and town of Saint-Pierre, the island's business center. After the eruption, much of the town was not rebuilt, and many ruins are still visible. The 4,583-foot-tall (1,397 m) volcanic mountain most recently erupted in 1929 but caused little damage.

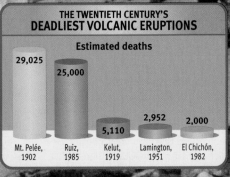

THE TWENTIETH CENTURY'S
DEADLIEST VOLCANIC ERUPTIONS

Estimated deaths

Mt. Pelée, 1902	Ruiz, 1985	Kelut, 1919	Lamington, 1951	El Chichón, 1982
29,025	25,000	5,110	2,952	2,000

Deadliest Twentieth-Century Hurricane

Hurricane Mitch

THE TWENTIETH CENTURY'S DEADLIEST HURRICANES

Estimated deaths

Hurricane Mitch, 1998	Galveston, Texas, 1900	Hurricane Fifi, 1974	Dominican Republic, 1930	Hurricane Flora, 1963
11,000	8,000	8,000	8,000	7,200

Beginning on October 26, 1998, Hurricane Mitch pounded Central America, killing more than 11,000 people and causing more than $3 billion in damage. The countries hit hardest were Nicaragua and Honduras, but El Salvador and Guatemala also sustained significant damage. At the peak of the storm, wind gusts reached up to 180 miles per hour (157 knots) and remained that way for 24 hours. Besides the gusting winds and pouring rain, giant mud slides and raging floods destroyed millions of homes and took thousands of lives.

World's
Deadliest Tsunami

Agadir, Morocco

On February 29, 1960, a tsunami created by a giant earthquake hit the small coastal town of Agadir, Morocco, and killed an estimated 12,000 people. Only about a quarter of this North African town survived the disaster. Since then, Agadir has rebuilt and become a popular tourist destination because of its sandy beaches and warm, sunny weather. A tsunami is a series of giant ocean waves that are caused by earthquakes, volcanic eruptions, or landslides. When a tsunami nears land, the waves may be as high as 100 feet (30.5 m).

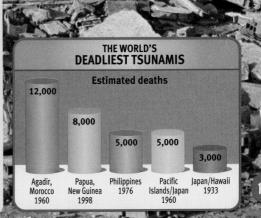

THE WORLD'S DEADLIEST TSUNAMIS

Estimated deaths

Agadir, Morocco 1960	Papua, New Guinea 1998	Philippines 1976	Pacific Islands/Japan 1960	Japan/Hawaii 1933
12,000	8,000	5,000	5,000	3,000

167

Country with the Most
Fast-Food Restaurants

There are approximately 554,170 fast-food restaurants in China, and many of them are less than 10 years old. The fast-food craze caught on in China because the restaurants are so much more affordable than many of the other eating places in the country. The most popular fast-food restaurant in China is KFC, followed by McDonald's, California Fried Chicken, and Pizza Hut. Some of the most popular Asian fast-food chains include Japan's Mos Burger and Hong Kong's Café de Coral.

COUNTRIES WITH THE MOST
FAST-FOOD RESTAURANTS

Number of restaurants

Country	Number
China	554,170
USA	177,125
India	38,598
Japan	38,429
UK	26,189

World's Largest Fruit

Pumpkin

Although the average size of a pumpkin can vary greatly depending on the variety and species, the greatest weight ever attained by a fruit belongs to a pumpkin. The largest pumpkin ever grown (and recorded) weighed a remarkable 1,061 pounds (481 kg). Pumpkins have a long tradition in the United States and were served at the first Thanksgiving. Today, pumpkins are used mainly in pies, soups, and puddings. People also carve faces in pumpkins on Halloween. In Europe, pumpkin is usually served as a meal's side dish.

THE WORLD'S LARGEST FRUITS

Maximum weight in pounds/kilograms

1,061 lb. 481.3 kg.	Pumpkin
50 lb. 22.7 kg.	Watermelon
32 lb. 14.5 kg.	Banana Squash
18 lb. 8.2 kg.	Indian Moschata Squash
9 lb. 4.0 kg.	Casaba Melon

169

World's
Largest Vegetable

Yam

True yams can consistently grow up to 9 feet (2.7 m) long and weigh more than 150 pounds (68 kg). Some specially grown vegetables have been recorded at higher weights than the largest yam, but no other vegetable can consistently reach this size and weight. Even though these giant tropical tuber roots are capable of reaching such a great size, they are usually harvested when they reach about 6 pounds (2.7 kg). While yams are a major food crop in several countries, some varieties

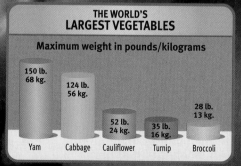

THE WORLD'S LARGEST VEGETABLES

Maximum weight in pounds/kilograms

Yam	Cabbage	Cauliflower	Turnip	Broccoli
150 lb. 68 kg.	124 lb. 56 kg.	52 lb. 24 kg.	35 lb. 16 kg.	28 lb. 13 kg.

Country That Eats the Most Chocolate

Switzerland

In Switzerland, the average person consumes about 26 pounds (11.8 kg) of chocolate each year. That means approximately 188 million pounds (85 million kg) of chocolate are eaten in this small country annually. Chocolate has always been a popular food around the world. In fact, each year, approximately 594,000 tons (538,758 t) of cocoa beans—an important ingredient in chocolate—are consumed worldwide. Chocolate is consumed mainly in the form of candy, but it is also used to make beverages, to flavor recipes, and to glaze various sweets and bakery products.

THE WORLD'S TOP CHOCOLATE-EATING COUNTRIES

Annual chocolate consumption per capita in pounds/kilograms

Switzerland	Liechtenstein	Luxembourg	UK	Belgium
25.4 lb. 11.5 kg.	22.9 lb. 10.4 kg.	22.7 lb. 10.3 kg.	21.6 lb. 9.8 kg.	18.9 lb. 8.6 kg.

Country That Eats the Most Meat

Each person in the United States will eat about 264 pounds (120 kg) of meat this year. That's the same weight as 75 phone books. Beef is the most commonly eaten meat in the United States. Each American eats about 63 pounds (29 kg) per year. In fact, an average 44.5 million pounds (20.2 million kg) of beef are eaten in the United States each day. The most common way to eat beef is in the form of a hamburger or cheeseburger. More than 85% of U.S. citizens ate one of these fast food items last year. Chicken is the second most popular meat, with each American eating about 59 pounds (26.8 kg) per year.

THE COUNTRIES WITH THE HIGHEST MEAT CONSUMPTION

Annual consumption per capita in pounds/kilograms

USA	Cyprus	New Zealand	Australia	Spain
264 lb. 120 kg.	252 lb. 114 kg.	242 lb. 110 kg.	238 lb. 108 kg.	237 lb. 108 kg.

Country That
Drinks the Most Tea

Ireland

Each person in Ireland drinks an average of 1,184 cups of tea each year. This means that the country's population goes through about 44.9 billion cups or 2.8 billion gallons (10.6 billion l) annually. Not surprisingly, tea shops are common in Ireland. The three main types of tea sold in the country are black, green, and oolong. Teas usually get their name from their color or place of origin. Green teas are mostly imported from China and Japan; black teas are from China, India, and Sri Lanka; and oolongs are mainly from Taiwan.

**THE WORLD'S
TOP TEA-DRINKING COUNTRIES**

Annual per capita consumption in cups

Ireland	Libya	Kuwait	Turkey	UK
1,184	1,074	1,069	1,056	1,025

Countries That Eat the Most Potato Chips

United Kingdom and United States

People in the United Kingdom and the United States eat a lot of chips—each averaging about 6.8 pounds (3.1 kg) per capita each year. This means that each person snacks on almost 14 bags in just 12 months, and some 8,500 million packages are sold each year! Better known as "crisps" in the United Kingdom, potato chips were first served in 1853 at a lodge in Saratoga Springs, New York. It takes about 10,000 pounds (4,540 kg) of potatoes to make 3,500 pounds (1,589 kg) of chips.

THE WORLD'S TOP POTATO CHIP-EATING COUNTRIES

Per capita consumption in pounds/kilograms

UK	USA	Iceland	New Zealand	Norway
6.8 lb. 3.1 kg.	6.8 lb. 3.1 kg.	5.9 lb. 2.7 kg.	5.9 lb. 2.7 kg.	5.7 lb. 2.6 kg.

Country That Eats the Most Ice Cream

Australia

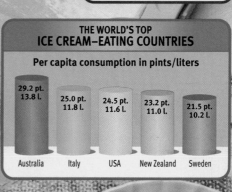

THE WORLD'S TOP ICE CREAM–EATING COUNTRIES

Per capita consumption in pints/liters

Australia	Italy	USA	New Zealand	Sweden
29.2 pt. 13.8 l.	25.0 pt. 11.8 l.	24.5 pt. 11.6 l.	23.2 pt. 11.0 l.	21.5 pt. 10.2 l.

Each year, the per capita consumption of ice cream in Australia is 29.2 pints (13.8 l). That averages to about 2.28 billion scoops of this frozen favorite for the nation. That means each person would have to eat about one cup a week during the entire year. Frozen desserts date back to the Roman Empire when people mixed mountain ice with fruit. Ice cream became popular in France, England, and the United States in the eighteenth century. The ice-cream cone was invented in 1904. Today, ice-cream sales total billions of dollars throughout the world.

Country That Consumes the Most Soft Drinks

United States

Americans have an annual per capita soft drink consumption of 377.9 pints (178.7 l). This means that each person in the country drinks an average of 504 cans of soda each year. Soda accounts for about 25% of all drinks consumed in the United States, and some 15 billion gallons (56.8 billion l) are sold annually. Recent studies show that diet sodas, as well as flavored sodas such as cherry, orange, and root beer, are becoming more popular than colas. The country's three top-selling soft-drink companies are the Coca-Cola Company, PepsiCo Inc., and Dr. Pepper/7 Up.

THE WORLD'S TOP SODA-DRINKING COUNTRIES

Per capita consumption in pints/liters

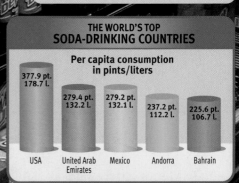

377.9 pt. 178.7 l.	279.4 pt. 132.2 l.	279.2 pt. 132.1 l.	237.2 pt. 112.2 l.	225.6 pt. 106.7 l.
USA	United Arab Emirates	Mexico	Andorra	Bahrain

Country That Eats the Most Fish

The Maldives

Per capita fish consumption in the Maldives averages 353.2 pounds (160.2 kg) each year. This means that all together, the population on this small nation of islands in the north Indian Ocean eats about 110 million pounds (50 million kg) of fish each year. Because the country consists of more than 1,000 coral islands, it makes sense that fishing is one of the top sources of food and income for the people living there. In addition to harvesting fish, Maldivians also eat corn and grains.

THE WORLD'S TOP FISH-EATING COUNTRIES

Per capita consumption in pounds/kilograms

Maldives	Iceland	Kiribati	Japan	Seychelles
353.2 lb. 160.2 kg.	202.2 lb. 91.7 kg.	170.2 lb. 77.2 kg.	159.2 lb. 72.2 kg.	142.8 lb. 64.8 kg.

World's Largest
Meteor Crater

Sudbury Crater

The Sudbury Crater in Ontario, Canada, measures 125 miles (200 km) in diameter. Scientists think it was created when a high-velocity comet the size of Mount Everest crashed into Earth 1.8 billion years ago. The force of this great impact melted a crater in the ground that is about six times the volume of Lake Huron and Lake Ontario combined. Scientists believe that this type of impact happens once every 350 years or so. The Sudbury Crater has suffered some 3.1 miles (5 km) of erosion over the years. The area is frequently used for mining because of the large deposits of copper and nickel found there.

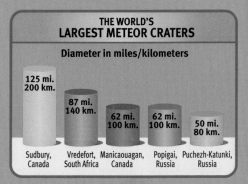

THE WORLD'S LARGEST METEOR CRATERS

Diameter in miles/kilometers

125 mi. 200 km.	87 mi. 140 km.	62 mi. 100 km.	62 mi. 100 km.	50 mi. 80 km.
Sudbury, Canada	Vredefort, South Africa	Manicaouagan, Canada	Popigai, Russia	Puchezh-Katunki, Russia

World's Tallest Mountain

Mount Everest

Towering 29,035 feet (8,850 m) into the air, Mt. Everest's tallest peak is the highest point on Earth. This peak is an unbelievable 5.5 miles (8.8 km) above sea level. Mt. Everest is located in the Himalayas, on the border between Nepal and Tibet. Although it is called Mother Goddess of the Land by Tibetans, the mountain got its official name from surveyor Sir George Everest. In 1953, Sir Edmund Hillary and Tenzing Norgay were the first people to reach the peak.

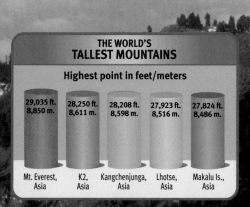

THE WORLD'S TALLEST MOUNTAINS

Highest point in feet/meters

Mt. Everest, Asia	K2, Asia	Kangchenjunga, Asia	Lhotse, Asia	Makalu Is., Asia
29,035 ft. 8,850 m.	28,250 ft. 8,611 m.	28,208 ft. 8,598 m.	27,923 ft. 8,516 m.	27,824 ft. 8,486 m.

World's Longest
Mountain Chain

The Andes

The Andes extend for about 5,000 miles (8,050 km) through seven countries of South America— Venezuela, Colombia, Ecuador, Peru, Bolivia, Chile, and Argentina. The Andes also have some of the highest peaks in the world, with more than fifty of them measuring above 20,000 feet (6,100 m). Some of the animals found in the Andes include wild horses; vicuñas—members of the camel family; and chinchillas, furry members of the rodent family. The condor—the world's largest bird of prey—also calls these mountains its home.

THE WORLD'S LONGEST MOUNTAIN CHAINS

Length in miles/kilometers

5,000 mi. 8,050 km.	2,200 mi. 3,542 km.	2,000 mi. 3,220 km.	1,900 mi. 3,059 km.	1,600 mi. 2,576 km.
Andes, South America	Trans-Antarctic Mountains, Antarctica	Rocky Mountains, USA	Great Dividing Range, Australia	Himalayas, Asia

World's Largest Ocean

Pacific

The Pacific Ocean covers almost 64 million square miles (166 million sq km) and reaches 36,200 feet (11,000 m) below sea level at its greatest depth—the Mariana Trench (near the Philippines). In fact, this ocean is so large that it covers about one-third of the planet (more than all of Earth's land put together) and holds more than half of all the seawater on Earth, about 6 sextillion (21 zeros) gallons (23 sextillion l). The United States could fit inside this ocean 18 times! Some of the major bodies of water included in the Pacific are the Bering Sea, the Coral Sea, the Philippine Sea, and the Gulf of Alaska.

THE WORLD'S LARGEST OCEANS

Maximum area in millions of square miles/square kilometers

Pacific Ocean	64 M sq. mi. / 165.7 M sq. km.
Atlantic Ocean	31.8 M sq. mi. / 82.4 M sq. km.
Indian Ocean	25.3 M sq. mi. / 65.5 M sq. km.
Arctic Ocean	5.4 M sq. mi. / 14.0 M sq. km.

181

World's
Largest Desert

The Sahara

THE WORLD'S LARGEST DESERTS

Area in millions of square miles/square kilometers

3.5 M sq. mi. 9.1 M sq. km.	1.4 M sq. mi. 3.6 M sq. km.	0.5 M sq. mi. 1.3 M sq. km.	0.4 M sq. mi. 1.0 M sq. km.	0.2 M sq. mi. 0.5 M sq. km.
Sahara, Africa	Australian, Australia	Arabian, Asia	Gobi, Africa	Kalahari, Africa

The Sahara Desert in northern Africa covers approximately 3.5 million square miles (9.1 million sq km). It stretches for 5,200 miles (8,372 km) through the countries of Morocco, Algeria, Tunisia, Libya, Egypt, Mauritania, Mali, Niger, Chad, and Sudan. The Sahara gets very little rainfall—less than 8 inches (20 cm) per year. Date palms and acacias grow near oases. Some of the animals that live in the Sahara include gazelles, antelopes, jackals, foxes, and badgers.

World's
Largest Lake

Caspian Sea

This giant inland body of saltwater stretches for almost 750 miles (1,207 km) from north to south, with an average width of about 200 miles (322 km). All together, it covers an area that's almost the same size as the state of California. The Caspian Sea is located east of the Caucasus Mountains in Central Asia. It is bordered by Iran, Russia, Kazakhstan, Azerbaijan, and Turkmenistan. The Caspian Sea has an average depth of about 550 feet (170 m). It is an important fishing resource, with species including sturgeon, salmon, perch, herring, and carp. Other animals live in the Caspian Sea, including porpoises, seals, and tortoises.

THE WORLD'S LARGEST LAKES

Approximate area in square miles/ square kilometers

Caspian Sea, Asia	Superior, N. America	Victoria, Africa	Huron, N. America	Michigan, N. America
143,205 sq. mi. 370,901 sq. km.	31,820 sq. mi. 82,413 sq. km.	26,570 sq. mi. 68,816 sq. km.	23,010 sq. mi. 59,596 sq. km.	22,400 sq. mi. 58,016 sq. km.

World's
Highest Waterfall

Angel Falls

Angel Falls is the world's highest waterfall at 3,212 feet (979 m). It also holds the record for the longest single drop of any waterfall at 2,648 feet (807 m). Angel Falls is located on the Churun River in the Guiana Highlands of southeastern Venezuela. As the upper river flows over the majestic cliffs, it takes 14 seconds for its water to plunge into the river below. Although rumors of this giant waterfall existed for many years, it was first documented by Ernesto Sanchez La Cruz in 1910. The falls were later named for an American bush pilot, Jimmy Angel, after he spotted them from the air.

THE WORLD'S
HIGHEST WATERFALLS

Height in feet/meters

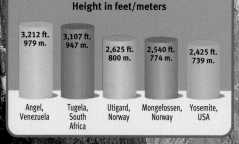

3,212 ft. 979 m.	3,107 ft. 947 m.	2,625 ft. 800 m.	2,540 ft. 774 m.	2,425 ft. 739 m.
Angel, Venezuela	Tugela, South Africa	Utigard, Norway	Mongefossen, Norway	Yosemite, USA

World's
Longest River

The Nile

**THE WORLD'S
LONGEST RIVERS**

Total length in miles/kilometers

Nile, Africa	4,145 mi. 6,671 km.
Amazon, S. America	4,000 mi. 6,437 km.
Mississippi-Missouri, N. America	3,740 mi. 6,021 km.
Yangtze, Asia	3,720 mi. 5,987 km.
Yenisei-Angara, Asia	3,650 mi. 5,877 km.

Flowing 4,145 miles (6,671 km), the Nile River in Africa stretches from the tributaries of Lake Victoria in Tanzania and Uganda out to the Mediterranean Sea. Because of varying depths, boats can sail on only about 2,000 miles (3,217 km) of the river. The Nile flows through Rwanda, Uganda, Sudan, and Egypt. The river's water supply is crucial to the existence of these African countries. The Nile's precious water is used to irrigate crops and to generate electricity. The Aswan Dam and the Aswan High Dam—both located in Egypt—are used to store the autumn floodwater for later use.

World's
Largest Rock

Ayers Rock

Ayers Rock shoots up 1,100 feet (335 m) above the surrounding desert. The oval-shaped rock is 2.2 miles (3.5 km) long and 1.5 miles (2.4 km) wide. Although it is not the tallest rock, Ayers Rock is the largest by volume. It is located in the southwestern section of the Northern Territory of Australia. Ayers Rock is officially owned by Australia's native people, the Aborigines, who consider the caves at its base to be sacred. The Aborigines lease the giant monolith to the national government so the public may visit it as part of Uluru National Park.

THE WORLD'S
LARGEST ROCKS

Height in feet/meters

1,100 ft. 335 m.	1,100 ft. 335 m.	1,024 ft. 312 m.	900 ft. 274 m.	571 ft. 174 m.
Ayers Rock, Australia	Dzyarzhynskay, Belarus	Gaizinakalns, Latvia	Seneca Rocks, USA	Coloane Alto, Macau

World's
Largest Island

Greenland

Greenland, located in the North Atlantic Ocean, covers more than 840,000 square miles (2,175,600 sq km). Not including continents, it is the largest island in the world. Its jagged coastline is approximately 24,400 miles (39,267 km) long—about the same distance as Earth's circumference at the equator. Mountain chains are located on Greenland's east and west coasts, and the coastline is indented by fjords, or thin bodies of water bordered by steep cliffs. From north to south, the island stretches for about 1,660 miles (2,670 km). About 700,000 square miles (1,813,000 sq km) of this massive island are covered by a giant ice sheet. Scientists have recently studied these ice sheets to learn more about the history of the world's changing climate.

THE WORLD'S LARGEST ISLANDS

Approximate area in square miles/square kilometers

Greenland	New Guinea	Borneo	Madagascar	Baffin Island
840,070 sq. mi. 2,175,600 sq. km.	312,190 sq. mi. 808,572 sq. km.	289,961 sq. mi. 751,000 sq. km.	226,674 sq. mi. 587,086 sq. km.	195,926 sq. mi. 507,448 sq. km.

World's
Highest Island

New Guinea

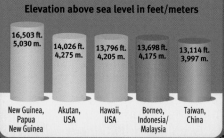

THE WORLD'S HIGHEST ISLANDS

Elevation above sea level in feet/meters

New Guinea, Papua New Guinea	Akutan, USA	Hawaii, USA	Borneo, Indonesia/ Malaysia	Taiwan, China
16,503 ft. 5,030 m.	14,026 ft. 4,275 m.	13,796 ft. 4,205 m.	13,698 ft. 4,175 m.	13,114 ft. 3,997 m.

New Guinea, an island that is part of the nation of Papua New Guinea, sits at an elevation of 16,503 feet (5,030 m) above sea level. It is also the second-largest island in the world. This tropical island has several giant mountain ranges, including the Owen Stanley and the Bismarck Mountains. Jaya Peak, located in Irian Jaya, is the highest point on the island. Some of the creatures that inhabit the island include tree kangaroos, spiny anteaters, and crocodiles. There are also about 650 bird species on the island.

World's Most Harvested Plant

Corn

Each year, the world harvests some 609 tons (552 t) of corn. The United States is the world's top corn-growing county, producing about 40% of the total corn crop. It is mostly grown in the country's Midwestern region, known as the Corn Belt. More than half the corn grown in the United States is used for livestock feed, about 25% of the crop is exported, and some 15% is sold as food. Brazil, China, and Mexico also grow a significant amount of corn. In South and Central America, corn is often ground by hand to make tortillas, tamales, and other staple dishes.

THE WORLD'S MOST HARVESTED PLANTS

Millions of tons/metric tons

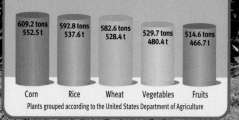

Corn	Rice	Wheat	Vegetables	Fruits
609.2 tons 552.5 t	592.8 tons 537.6 t	582.6 tons 528.4 t	529.7 tons 480.4 t	514.6 tons 466.7 t

Plants grouped according to the United States Department of Agriculture

World's
Largest Seed

Coco de Mer

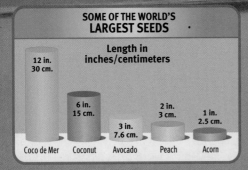

SOME OF THE WORLD'S LARGEST SEEDS

Length in inches/centimeters

Coco de Mer	Coconut	Avocado	Peach	Acorn
12 in. 30 cm.	6 in. 15 cm.	3 in. 7.6 cm.	2 in. 3 cm.	1 in. 2.5 cm.

The giant, dark brown seed of the coco de mer palm tree can reach 12 inches (30 cm) long, measure 3 feet (1 m) in diameter, and weigh up to 40 pounds (18 kg). Only a few thousand seeds are produced each year. Coco de mer trees are found on the island of Praslin in the Seychelles Archipelago of the Indian Ocean. The area where some of the few remaining trees grow has been declared a Natural World Heritage Site in an effort to protect the species from poachers looking for the rare seeds. The tree can grow up to 100 feet (31 m) tall, with leaves measuring 20 feet (6 m) long and 12 feet (3.6 m) wide.

Country That Produces the Most Fruit

China

Each year, China produces more than 62 tons (56 t) of fruit—about 14% of the world's total fruit production. The country's fruit crop is worth about $12.2 billion annually. China is the world's top producer of apples and pears, and ranks third in the world for citrus fruit production. The country's orchards total about 21.5 million acres (8.6 M ha)—almost a quarter of the world's orchard land. More than half of China's population works in the agriculture industry.

COUNTRIES THAT PRODUCE THE MOST FRUIT

Tons/metric tons produced annually

China	India	Brazil	USA	Italy
62.3 tons 56.5 t	48.8 tons 44.3 t	39.7 tons 36.0 t	33.9 tons 30.7 t	21.3 tons 19.3 t

World's
Largest Flower

Rafflesia

THE WORLD'S LARGEST FLOWERS

Maximum flower size in inches/centimeters

36 in. 91 cm.				
	19 in. 48 cm.	18 in. 46 cm.	14 in. 36 cm.	10 in. 25 cm.
Rafflesia	Sunflower	Giant Water Lily	Brazilian Dutchman	Magnolia

The giant rafflesia, also known as the "stinking corpse lily," has blossoms that can reach 3 feet (1 m) in diameter and weigh up to 25 pounds (11 kg). Its petals can grow 1.5 feet (0.5 m) long and 1 inch (2.5 cm) thick. There are 16 different species of Rafflesia. This endangered plant is found only in the rain forests of Borneo and Sumatra. It lives inside the bark of host vines and is noticeable only when its flowers break through to blossom. The large, reddish-purple flowers give off a smell similar to rotting meat, which attracts insects to help spread the rafflesia's pollen.

World's Deadliest Plant

Castor Bean Plant

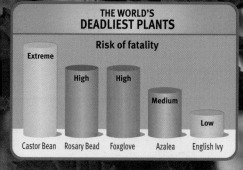

THE WORLD'S DEADLIEST PLANTS

Risk of fatality

Castor Bean	Rosary Bead	Foxglove	Azalea	English Ivy
Extreme	High	High	Medium	Low

The seeds of the castor bean plant contain a protein called ricin. Scientists estimate that ricin is about 6,000 times more poisonous than cyanide and 12,000 times more poisonous than rattlesnake venom. It would take a particle of ricin only about the size of a grain of sand to kill a 160-pound (73-kg) adult. The deadly beans are actually quite pretty and are sometimes used in jewelry. Castor bean plants grow in warmer climates and can reach a height of about 10 feet (3 m). Its leaves can measure up to 2 feet (0.6 m) wide.

World's Tallest Weed

Giant Hogweed

The giant hogweed can grow to a height of 12 feet (3.6 m) and have leaves that measure 3 feet (91 cm) long. That's taller than some trees. The giant hogweed is part of the parsley or carrot family and it has hollow stalks with tiny white flowers. Although it was first brought to America from Asia as an ornamental plant, the hogweed quickly became a pest. Each plant can produce about 50,000 seeds and the weed quickly spreads through its environment.

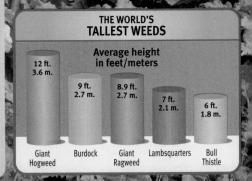

THE WORLD'S TALLEST WEEDS

Average height in feet/meters

12 ft. 3.6 m.	9 ft. 2.7 m.	8.9 ft. 2.7 m.	7 ft. 2.1 m.	6 ft. 1.8 m.
Giant Hogweed	Burdock	Giant Ragweed	Lambsquarters	Bull Thistle

World's Most
Poisonous Mushroom

Death Cap

THE WORLD'S
MOST POISONOUS MUSHROOMS

**Ranked 1–5 by likeliness to
cause death in humans**

1. Death Cap
2. Destroying Angel
3. Amanita Alba
4. Fly Agaric
5. Deadly Galerina

Among the most dangerous mushrooms are members of the Amanita family, which includes Destroying Angels and the highly dangerous Amanita phalloides, or Death Cap. The Death Cap contains deadly peptide toxins that cause rapid loss of bodily fluids and intense thirst. Within six hours, the poison shuts down the kidneys, liver, and central nervous system, causing coma and—in more than 50% of cases—death. Estimates of the number of poisonous mushroom species range from 80 to 2,000. Most experts agree, however, that at least 100 varieties will cause severe symptoms and even death if eaten.

World's
Tallest Cactus

Saguaro

Although most saguaro cacti grow to a height of 50 feet (15 m), some have actually reached 75 feet (23 m). That's taller than a seven-story building. Saguaros start out quite small and grow very slowly. A saguaro only reaches about 1 inch (2.5 cm) high during its first 10 years. It will not bloom until it is between 50 and 75 years old. By this time, the cactus has a strong root system that can support about 9 to 10 tons (8 to 9 t) of growth. Its spines can measure up to 2.5 inches (5 cm) long. The giant cactus can be found from southeastern California to southern Arizona.

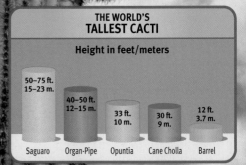

THE WORLD'S TALLEST CACTI

Height in feet/meters

Saguaro	Organ-Pipe	Opuntia	Cane Cholla	Barrel
50–75 ft. 15–23 m.	40–50 ft. 12–15 m.	33 ft. 10 m.	30 ft. 9 m.	12 ft. 3.7 m.

World's
Largest Leaves

Raffia Palm

Reaching lengths of 65 feet (19.8 m) long, the leaves of these tropical palms measure about the same length as a regulation tennis court. Raffia trees have several stems that can reach heights of 6 to 30 feet (2 to 9 m). When they reach about 50 years of age, raffia palms flower and produce egg-size fruits covered in hard scales. Several products come from these palms, including raffia and floor and shoe polish. Raffia leaves are also used to weave baskets, mats, and hats. These enormous plants are native to Madagascar, but can also be found along Africa's eastern coast.

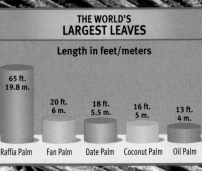

THE WORLD'S
LARGEST LEAVES

Length in feet/meters

Raffia Palm	Fan Palm	Date Palm	Coconut Palm	Oil Palm
65 ft. 19.8 m.	20 ft. 6 m.	18 ft. 5.5 m.	16 ft. 5 m.	13 ft. 4 m.

World's Tallest Tree

California Redwood

California redwoods, which grow in both California and southern Oregon, can reach 385 feet (117.4 m) in height. Their trunks can grow up to 25 feet (7.6 m) in diameter. The tallest recorded redwood stands 385 feet (117.4 m) tall—more than 60 feet (18.3 m) taller than the Statue of Liberty. Some redwoods are believed to be more than 2,000 years old. The trees' thick bark and foliage protect them from natural hazards such as insects and fires.

THE WORLD'S TALLEST TREE SPECIES

Height in feet/meters

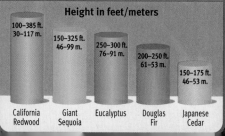

100–385 ft. 30–117 m.	150–325 ft. 46–99 m.	250–300 ft. 76–91 m.	200–250 ft. 61–53 m.	150–175 ft. 46–53 m.
California Redwood	Giant Sequoia	Eucalyptus	Douglas Fir	Japanese Cedar

Place with the World's Fastest Winds

Mount Washington

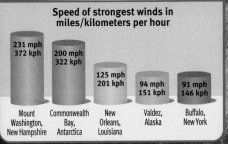

THE WORLD'S FASTEST WINDS

Speed of strongest winds in miles/kilometers per hour

231 mph 372 kph	200 mph 322 kph	125 mph 201 kph	94 mph 151 kph	91 mph 146 kph
Mount Washington, New Hampshire	Commonwealth Bay, Antarctica	New Orleans, Louisiana	Valdez, Alaska	Buffalo, New York

In 1934, winds at the top of Mount Washington reached a world record of 231 miles (372 km) per hour—and these gusts were not part of a storm. Normally, the average wind speed at the summit of this mountain is approximately 36 miles (58 km) per hour. Located in the White Mountains of New Hampshire, Mount Washington is the highest peak in New England at 6,288 feet (1,917 m). The treeless summit, which is known for its harsh weather, has an average annual temperature of only 26.5° Fahrenheit (-3.1° C).

World's Driest
Inhabited Place

Aswan

Aswan, Egypt, receives an average rainfall of only .02 inches (.5 mm) per year. In the country's sunniest and southernmost city, summer temperatures can reach a blistering 114° Fahrenheit (46° C). Aswan is located on the west bank of the Nile River. The Aswan High Dam, at 12,565 feet (3,830 m) long, is the city's most famous landmark. It produces the majority of Egypt's power in the form of hydroelectricity. Aswan also has many Pharaonic, Greco-Roman, and Muslim ruins.

THE WORLD'S DRIEST INHABITED PLACES

Average annual rainfall in inches/millimeters

Aswan, Egypt	Luxar, Egypt	Arica, Chile	Ica, Peru	Antofagasta, Chile
0.02 in. 0.50 mm.	0.03 in. 0.76 mm.	0.04 in. 1.0 mm.	0.09 in. 2.3 mm.	0.19 in. 4.8 mm

World's Wettest
Inhabited Place

Buenaventura

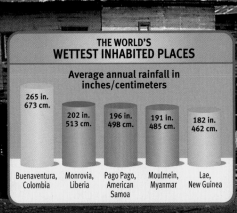

THE WORLD'S WETTEST INHABITED PLACES

Average annual rainfall in inches/centimeters

265 in. 673 cm.	202 in. 513 cm.	196 in. 498 cm.	191 in. 485 cm.	182 in. 462 cm.
Buenaventura, Colombia	Monrovia, Liberia	Pago Pago, American Samoa	Moulmein, Myanmar	Lae, New Guinea

Near the thick South American jungles on the Pacific coast of Colombia, the city of Buenaventura receives an average rainfall of 265 inches (673 cm) each year. That depth is equivalent to the height of a 2-story building. This city is best known for its shipping—it is home to Colombia's most important Pacific port. Each year, the port of Buenaventura receives corn, wheat, fertilizers, vehicles, and many other important goods. It also ships out many of Colombia's major agricultural products, including coffee, sugar, and molasses.

World's Hottest
Inhabited Place

Djibouti

Located on the continent of Africa, Djibouti is the capital of the Republic of Djibouti. During the hottest months, which are May through September, the monthly average temperature can reach 99° Fahrenheit (37° C) in this port city. Even in the cool season, temperatures may reach above 85° Fahrenheit (30° C). Djibouti's climate is very dry, and few plant species survive there. There is little rainfall, and there are no surface rivers or streams that flow year-round. Most of the nation's water is supplied by the Houmbouli River, which flows underground.

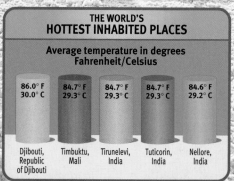

THE WORLD'S
HOTTEST INHABITED PLACES

Average temperature in degrees Fahrenheit/Celsius

Djibouti, Republic of Djibouti	Timbuktu, Mali	Tirunelevi, India	Tuticorin, India	Nellore, India
86.0° F 30.0° C	84.7° F 29.3° C	84.7° F 29.3° C	84.7° F 29.3° C	84.6° F 29.2° C

World's Coldest Inhabited Place

Norilsk

Norilsk—a small city located in the Rybnaya Valley of central Russia—has an average temperature of only 12.4° Fahrenheit (-10.9° C). That's an average of 20° Fahrenheit (-6.6° C) below freezing. Due to its extreme weather, it's not surprising that the city's population is only about 170,00 residents. Norilsk is north of the Arctic Circle, which accounts for its many days of freezing weather. The city also experiences five months without sunlight because of its location.

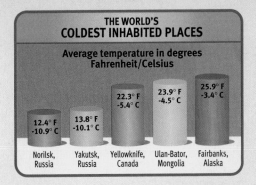

THE WORLD'S COLDEST INHABITED PLACES

Average temperature in degrees Fahrenheit/Celsius

Norilsk, Russia	Yakutsk, Russia	Yellowknife, Canada	Ulan-Bator, Mongolia	Fairbanks, Alaska
12.4° F -10.9° C	13.8° F -10.1° C	22.3° F -5.4° C	23.9° F -4.5° C	25.9° F -3.4° C

World's
Greatest Snowfall

Mount Rainier

Between 1971 and 1972, Mount Rainier had a record snowfall of 1,224 inches (3,109 cm). That's enough snow to cover a 10-story building! Located in the Cascade Mountains of Washington state, Mount Rainier is actually a volcano buried under 35 square miles (90.7 sq km) of snow and ice. The mountain, which covers about 100 square miles (259 sq km), reaches a height of 14,410 feet (4,392 m). Its three peaks include Liberty Cap, Point Success, and Columbia Crest. Mt. Rainier National Park was established in 1899.

THE WORLD'S
GREATEST ANNUAL SNOWFALLS

Highest annual snowfall
in inches/centimeters

1,224 in. 3,109 cm.	1,140 in. 2,895 cm.	1,122 in. 2,849 cm.	974 in. 2,474 cm.	964 in. 2,449 cm.
Mount Rainier, Washington, 1971–1972	Mount Baker, Washington, 1998–1999	Paradise Station, Washington, 1971–1972	Thompson Pass, Alaska, 1952–1953	Mount Copeland, British Columbia, 1971–1972

U.S. Records

Alabama to Wyoming

State with the World's Largest
Motorcycle Museum

Alabama

The Barber Vintage Motorsports Museum in Birmingham, Alabama, has a collection of almost 750 motorcycles. Of that 750, the museum only displays about 375 of them at one time. Some of the bikes that are not on display may be on loan to other museums or exhibits. The other bikes are stored at the museum or they may be continuously rotated into new displays. The Barber has motorcycles from all over the world and from every decade of the twentieth century. The museum opened to the public in 1995 in an effort to preserve the history of motorcycles.

THE WORLD'S
LARGEST MOTORCYCLE MUSEUMS

Average number of motorcycles on display

375	300	250	150	55
Barber Vintage Motorsports, Alabama	National Motorcycle Museum, Australia	Trev Deeley Museum, British Columbia	Sammy Miller Museum, England	Rocky Mountain Motorcycle Museum, Colorado

State with the Largest
National Park

Alaska

THE UNITED STATES'
LARGEST NATIONAL PARKS

Millions of acres/hectares

Park	Acres / Hectares
Wrangell-St. Elias, Alaska	8.32 M ac. / 3.35 M ha.
Gates of the Arctic, Alaska	7.52 M ac. / 3.04 M ha.
Denali, Alaska	4.74 M ac. / 1.92 M ha.
Katmai, Alaska	3.67 M ac. / 1.48 M ha.
Death Valley, California	3.28 M ac. / 1.32 M ha.

Wrangell-St. Elias National Park in Alaska measures more than 8.3 million acres (3.4 million ha), making it the largest national park in the United States. The Chugach, Wrangell, and St. Elias mountain ranges are all located here, and the area is nicknamed the "mountain kingdom of North America." Many mountain peaks are above 16,000 feet (4,880 m), including Mt. Elias—the United States' second largest peak—at 18,008 feet (5,492 m). The surrounding area consists of rivers, valleys, and glaciers. There is also a wide variety of wildlife in the region. The area was designated a World Heritage Site in 1980 and was declared a national park later that same year.

207

State with the World's
Sunniest Place

Arizona

The little town of Yuma, Arizona, enjoys bright, sunny days approximately 93% of the year. That means that the sun is shining about 339 days out of each year! Yuma is located in southwestern Arizona near the borders of California and Mexico. Although the temperatures are normally in the 70s year-round, the dry desert air keeps the humidity low. This climate, combined with the waters of the Colorado River, provide Yuma with an excellent environment for its thriving, $700 million-per-year agricultural business.

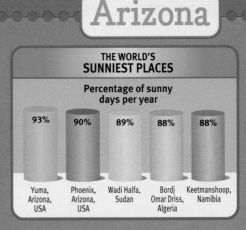

THE WORLD'S SUNNIEST PLACES

Percentage of sunny days per year

93%	90%	89%	88%	88%
Yuma, Arizona, USA	Phoenix, Arizona, USA	Wadi Halfa, Sudan	Bordj Omar Driss, Algeria	Keetmanshoop, Namibia

State with the Largest
Retail Headquarters

Arkansas

Wal-Mart—headquartered in Bentonville, Arkansas—logged $246.5 billion in sales in 2002. The company was founded in 1962 by Arkansas native Sam Walton, who saw his small variety stores grow into giant grocery stores, membership warehouse clubs, and deep-discount warehouse outlets. Wal-Mart currently employs 962,000 workers in the United States and 282,000 workers internationally. Walton's original store in Bentonville now serves as the company's visitor center.

THE UNITED STATES' LARGEST RETAIL HEADQUARTERS

Sales in billions of US dollars

Wal-Mart, Arkansas	Home Depot, Georgia	Kroger, Ohio	Target, Minnesota	Sears Roebuck, Illinois
$246.5 B	$58.2 B	$51.4 B	$43.9 B	$41.4 B

State with the World's
Largest Movie Studio

California

In Los Angeles, California, Universal City's Back Lot measures 420 acres (170 ha), making it the largest movie studio in the world. That's enough land to fit about 20 professional-size football stadiums! The site has 34 sound stages and 561 buildings. The Back Lot has a wide variety of theaters and sets, ranging from street scenes of Paris, London, New York, and the Old West to tropical lagoons. Universal Studios Theme Park is also located here and lets visitors tour sound stages that were used to film hit movies such as *The Scorpion King*, *Shrek*, *Jurassic Park*, and *The Mummy*.

THE WORLD'S LARGEST MOVIE STUDIOS

Size in acres/hectares

420 ac / 170 ha — Back Lot at Universal City California,

100 ac / 40.5 ha — Warner Brothers Studio, California

69 ac / 27.9 ha — Changchun Film Studio, China

44 ac / 17.8 ha — Walt Disney Studios, California

20 ac / 8.1 ha — Stapleton Studios, New York

State's Baseball Team with the Highest Seasonal Attendance

Colorado

In 1993, the seasonal attendance for the Colorado Rockies was an impressive 4.48 million fans. The Rockies finished up their inaugural season in October of the same year with the most wins by a National League expansion team. The Rockies played at Mile High Stadium for their first two years, and during their 135 games there, averaged a crowd of about 57,051 per game. The team moved to Denver's Coors Field in 1995 and proceeded to sell out 203 consecutive games. Since then, the new 76-acre (30.7-ha) ballpark has been a league leader in attendance.

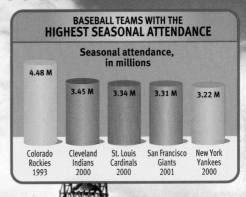

BASEBALL TEAMS WITH THE HIGHEST SEASONAL ATTENDANCE

Seasonal attendance, in millions

4.48 M	3.45 M	3.34 M	3.31 M	3.22 M
Colorado Rockies 1993	Cleveland Indians 2000	St. Louis Cardinals 2000	San Francisco Giants 2001	New York Yankees 2000

State with the Oldest Newspaper

Connecticut

LEMENS GETS WIN NO. 298; RAMIREZ HELPS RED SOX DEFEAT TWINS · SPORT

Hartford ⚜ Courant.

1N/5/6/7★ Spe

SUNDAY, MAY 11, 2003

ER 131   COPYRIGHT 2003, THE HARTFORD COURANT CO.

dustry Routinely Provides Incorrect Information
e Companies Know It. It's All Part Of The System

The *Hartford Courant*, which was started as a weekly paper in 1764 by Thomas Green, is actually older than the United States. In fact, George Washington placed an ad in the *Courant* to lease part of his Mount Vernon land. Noah Webster's "Blue-Backed Speller" was first published in this newspaper. And Thomas Jefferson sued the *Courant* for libel, but lost the case. The *Hartford Courant* became a daily paper in 1837, and its Sunday edition began in 1913. Today, the newspaper has a circulation of more than 200,000 daily and 300,000 for the Sunday edition.

so seriously flawed that costly re inevitable. A much-heralded sional reform effort seven years done little to repair the broken or to hold credit bureaus ac- ble, the investigation found. a system that forces hundreds of nds of consumers to overpay for ages, credit cards and even car operty insurance. And it rewards lustry for its own mistakes, deliv- millions in profits from selling reports to nervous consumers. rors seep into the system at every level.

Banks, credit card companies and de- partment stores might send incorrect or outdated account information to the massive credit bureaus. When bureaus assemble credit reports, they rely on in- exact computer matches that can easily mix consumers' records.

"Too many credit reports are a tick- ing time bomb of inaccurate informa- tion," said Ed Mierzwinski, consumer program director at the U.S. Public In- terest Research Group in Washington, D.C. "Consumers pay the price for the

PLEASE SEE **ERRORS**, PAGE A10

Courant has found that the credit reporting business is built on a

For Consul

*irst of two J

ENNETH R. (MATTHEW W URANT STAFF

andall tho ntil compl owerful decided bles. lived 50 m led for ban mes. Their street addresses ly identical. But they lived in towns, with different birth

Down East

Officials, omasso inked In Venture

212

Company Reportedly Planned Retail Center

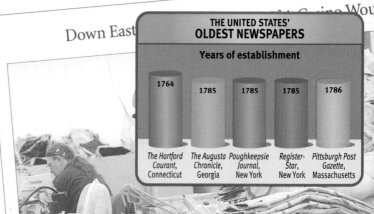

THE UNITED STATES' OLDEST NEWSPAPERS

Years of establishment

1764	1785	1785	1785	1786
The Hartford Courant, Connecticut	The Augusta Chronicle, Georgia	Poughkeepsie Journal, New York	Register-Star, New York	Pittsburgh Post Gazette, Massachusetts

State with the
Oldest Church

Delaware

THE UNITED STATES'
OLDEST CHURCHES

Year of establishment

Old Swedes Church, Delaware	Old Naragansett Church, Rhode Island	St. Francis Xavier Church, Maryland	New Hempstead Church, New York	Oak Grove Baptist Church, Virginia
1699	1707	1731	1734	1762

Old Swedes Church in Wilmington, Delaware, was built in 1699. First established as a Swedish Lutheran church, it is the nation's oldest church building still standing in its original form. The church's cemetery, a plot that was first used in 1638, is believed to hold many of Delaware's first settlers. In fact, when the church was constructed near the cemetery, the foundation was built around a number of early plots giving it an unusual shape. Old Swedes Church was designated a National Historic Landmark in 1963.

213

State with the
Tallest Hotel

Florida

The Four Seasons Hotel in Miami, Florida, towers a grand 788 feet (241 m) above the surrounding city landscape. This premium hotel has 182 guest rooms and 39 suites. Guests can enjoy a giant spa and health club, a beauty salon, and three swimming pools. The hotel also caters to younger visitors with bedtime milk and cookies, video games, and child-size robes. There is also a Kids for All Seasons program with arts and crafts, movies, and board games.

THE UNITED STATES' TALLEST HOTELS

Height in feet/meters

Four Seasons, Florida	Westin Peachtree, Georgia	Marriott Renaissance, Michigan	Four Seasons, New York	New York New York, Nevada
788 ft. 241 m.	723 ft. 220 m.	720 ft. 219 m.	682 ft. 208 m.	529 ft. 161 m.

State That Produces the
Most Peanuts

Georgia

Each year, Georgia produces a crop of peanuts weighing more than 1.3 billion pounds (590 million kg)! That's almost 50% of the nation's total peanut production. Farmers in the state harvest approximately 520,000 acres (210,441 ha) of peanut plants on more than 4,700 farms. About 60% of the peanuts exported overseas are from Georgia, generating about $150 million for the United States. Georgia's crop also makes up about one-half of the nuts used to make peanut butter.

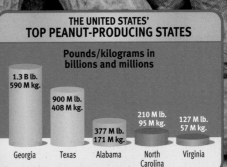

THE UNITED STATES'
TOP PEANUT-PRODUCING STATES

Pounds/kilograms in billions and millions

Georgia	Texas	Alabama	North Carolina	Virginia
1.3 B lb. 590 M kg.	900 M lb. 408 M kg.	377 M lb. 171 M kg.	210 M lb. 95 M kg.	127 M lb. 57 M kg.

State with the World's
Wettest Place

Hawaii

Mount Waialeale, located on the island of Kauai in Hawaii, receives about 460 inches (1,168 cm) of rain each year! Waialeale is located on Alakai Swamp—a plateau on the side of an extinct volcanic depression. It is 5,148 feet (1,569 m) high and is often surrounded by rain clouds. In 1982, Waialeale received 666 inches (1,692 cm) of rain and set an all-time world record. Over time, the constant rain has eroded gorges into the landscape, such as Waimea Canyon, which is 3,000 feet (915 m) deep.

**THE UNITED STATES'
WETTEST PLACES**

Annual rainfall in
inches/centimeters

Mt. Waialeale, Hawaii	Mobile, Alabama	New Orleans, Louisiana	Miami, Florida	Charleston, South Carolina
460 in. 1,168 cm.	86 in. 218 cm.	79 in. 201 cm.	70 in. 178 cm.	67 in. 170 cm.

State with the Largest
Raptor Habitat

Idaho

The Snake River Birds of Prey National Conservation Area is located along 81 miles (130 km) of the Snake River in Idaho. This rugged land is home to approximately 2,500 nesting raptors, or birds of prey. The birds stay there from mid-March until late June. Nesting raptor species found here include golden eagles, red-tailed hawks, barn owls, and turkey vultures. In addition to its many bird residents, the area also has one of the largest populations of badgers in the world. Congress designated the 601,053-acre (243,426 ha) habitat a National Conservation Area in August 1993.

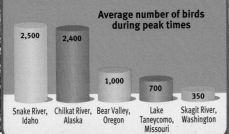

THE UNITED STATES'
LARGEST RAPTOR HABITATS

Average number of birds during peak times

Snake River, Idaho	Chilkat River, Alaska	Bear Valley, Oregon	Lake Taneycomo, Missouri	Skagit River, Washington
2,500	2,400	1,000	700	350

State with the Tallest Building

Illinois

The Sears Tower is the world's second-tallest inhabitable building. It is located in Chicago and rises 1,450 feet (442 m) above the ground. If you include the spires, the total height of the building grows to 1,707 feet (520 m). That's one-quarter of a mile high. It has 110 floors and 4.5 million square feet (400,000 sq m) of office space. If this floor space was laid out on one level, it would cover 16 city blocks. The Sears Tower weighs more than 222,500 tons (201,852 t) and cost $160 million to build.

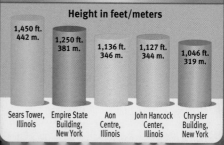

THE UNITED STATES' TALLEST BUILDINGS

Height in feet/meters

Building	Height
Sears Tower, Illinois	1,450 ft. 442 m.
Empire State Building, New York	1,250 ft. 381 m.
Aon Centre, Illinois	1,136 ft. 346 m.
John Hancock Center, Illinois	1,127 ft. 344 m.
Chrysler Building, New York	1,046 ft. 319 m.

State with the Largest
Children's Museum

Indiana

The Children's Museum of Indianapolis is a giant, 356,000-square-foot (33,072.4-sq-m) facility on 13 acres (5.3 ha) that houses 10 major galleries, including Scienceworks, Playscape, Passport to the World, and Mysteries in History. The Biotechnology Learning Center is an exciting new addition to the museum that teaches visitors about humans using living tools to meet their needs. Every year, families from all corners of the United States and Canada—approximately 1 million people—come to experience the wide variety of kid-friendly exhibits.

THE UNITED STATES'
LARGEST CHILDREN'S MUSEUMS

Size in square feet/ square meters

Museum	Size
Children's Museum of Indianapolis, Indiana	356,000 sq. ft. / 33,072 sq. m.
Port Discovery, Maryland	80,000 sq. ft. / 7,432 sq. m.
Chicago Children's Museum, Illinois	57,000 sq. ft. / 5,295 sq. m.
The Children's Museum, Washington	32,200 sq. ft. / 2,991 sq. m.
Garden State Discovery Museum, New Jersey	20,000 sq. ft. / 1,858 sq. m.

State That Produces the
Most Corn

Iowa

Each year, Iowa farmers grow about 1.72 billion bushels (.61 billion hl) of corn! That's enough to give each person in the United States about 6 bushels (2.1 hl) of corn. Level land and rich soil provide Iowa with the perfect farming environment. In fact, the state produces 10% of the nation's total food supply. Most of this state's corn, however, is raised for livestock feed. Iowa's corn-fed cattle and hogs are another large source of Iowa's income. Some of Iowa's corn is sold to make food products— the state is a major producer of popcorn.

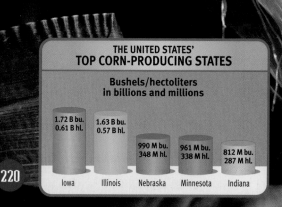

THE UNITED STATES'
TOP CORN-PRODUCING STATES

Bushels/hectoliters
in billions and millions

Iowa	Illinois	Nebraska	Minnesota	Indiana
1.72 B bu. 0.61 B hl.	1.63 B bu. 0.57 B hl.	990 M bu. 348 M hl.	961 M bu. 338 M hl.	812 M bu. 287 M hl.

State with the Largest
Ball of Twine

Kansas

In Cawker City, Kansas, there is a giant ball of twine that has a 40-foot (12-m) circumference and weighs more than 17,000 pounds (7,711 kg). The ball is 11 feet (3.4 m) tall and is made up of 1,140 miles (1,835 km) of twine. Frank Stoeber created the ball on his farm in 1953 from twine that he used to wrap hay bales. Cawker City assumed ownership of the twine ball in 1961 and holds a twine-a-thon each year in conjunction with the annual picnic. Thousands of feet of twine are added annually by the town's 800 residents and curious tourists.

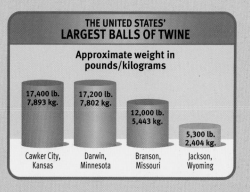

THE UNITED STATES'
LARGEST BALLS OF TWINE

Approximate weight in pounds/kilograms

17,400 lb. 7,893 kg.	17,200 lb. 7,802 kg.	12,000 lb. 5,443 kg.	5,300 lb. 2,404 kg.
Cawker City, Kansas	Darwin, Minnesota	Branson, Missouri	Jackson, Wyoming

State with the World's
Longest Cave System

Kentucky

With a complex system of tunnels that extends for more than 350 miles (563 km), Kentucky's Mammoth Cave is truly gigantic. Some scientists believe there are still sections of the cave yet to be discovered. This giant underground world has fascinated visitors since prehistoric times. In fact, many ancient artifacts and tools have been located there. Today, about 500,000 people visit the cave each year. They marvel at the stalagmite formations, bottomless pits, and underground rooms. Animals are also drawn to Mammoth Cave. About 130 different species can be found there, including bats, salamanders, and many types of insects.

THE WORLD'S
LONGEST CAVE SYSTEMS

Length in miles/kilometers

352 mi. 567 km.	125 mi. 201 km.	108 mi. 174 km.	103 mi. 166 km.	100 mi. 161 km.
Mammoth Cave, Kentucky	Optimisti- ceskaja, Ukraine	Jewel Cave, South Dakota	Holloch, Switzerland	Lechuguilla Cave, New Mexico

State with the Largest Alligator Population

Louisiana

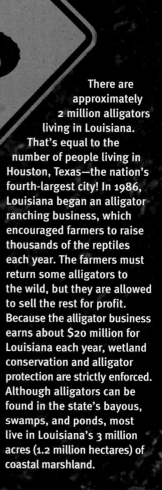

There are approximately 2 million alligators living in Louisiana. That's equal to the number of people living in Houston, Texas—the nation's fourth-largest city! In 1986, Louisiana began an alligator ranching business, which encouraged farmers to raise thousands of the reptiles each year. The farmers must return some alligators to the wild, but they are allowed to sell the rest for profit. Because the alligator business earns about $20 million for Louisiana each year, wetland conservation and alligator protection are strictly enforced. Although alligators can be found in the state's bayous, swamps, and ponds, most live in Louisiana's 3 million acres (1.2 million hectares) of coastal marshland.

GATOR XING NEXT 1/2 MILE

THE UNITED STATES' LARGEST ALLIGATOR POPULATIONS

Total number of alligators in millions/thousands

Louisiana	Florida	Texas	Georgia	Alabama
2.0 M	1.6 M	220,000	80,000	60,000

State with the Oldest State Fair

Maine

The first Skowhegan State Fair took place in 1819—a year before Maine officially became a state! Originally sponsored by the Somerset Central Agricultural Society, the fair name became official in 1842. State fairs were very important in the early 1900s. With no agricultural colleges in existence, fairs became the best way for farmers to learn about new agricultural methods and equipment. Today the Skowhegan State Fair features more than 7,000 exhibitors and performers, and people come from all over the country to enjoy concerts, livestock exhibits, and arts and crafts.

THE UNITED STATES' OLDEST STATE FAIRS

Year fair first held

Skowhegan State Fair, Maine	Three County Fair, Maine	Bangor State Fair, Maine	Brooklyn Fair, Connecticut	Woodstock Fair, Vermont
1819	1820	1851	1851	1862

State with the
Oldest Airport

Maryland

Wright brothers exhibit at
museum at College Park Airport

THE UNITED STATES'
OLDEST AIRPORTS

Year opened

1909	1911	1920	1921	1924
College Park Airport, Maryland	Robertson Airport, Connecticut	Hartness State Airport, Vermont	Bell County Airport, Kentucky	Page Field, Florida

The Wright brothers founded College Park Airport in 1909 to teach Army officers how to fly and it has been in operation ever since. The airport is now owned by the Maryland-National Capital Park and Planning Commission and is on the Register of Historic Places. Many aviation "firsts" occurred at this airport, such as the first woman passenger in the United States (1909), the first test of a bomb-dropping device (1911), the first U.S. Air Mail Service (1918),and the first controlled helicopter flight (1924).

225

State with the Oldest
Baseball Stadium

Massachusetts

Fenway Park opened its doors to baseball fans on April 20, 1912. The Boston Red Sox—the park's home team—won the World Series that year. The park is also the home of the Green Monster—a giant 37-foot (11.3-m) wall with an additional 23-foot (7-m) screen that has plagued home-run hitters since the park first opened. A seat out in the right-field bleachers is painted red to mark where the longest measurable home-run hit inside the park landed. It measured 502 feet (153 m) and was hit by Ted Williams in 1946.

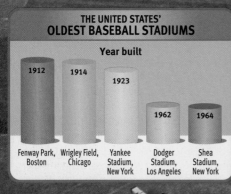

THE UNITED STATES'
OLDEST BASEBALL STADIUMS

Year built

1912	1914	1923	1962	1964
Fenway Park, Boston	Wrigley Field, Chicago	Yankee Stadium, New York	Dodger Stadium, Los Angeles	Shea Stadium, New York

BOSTON RED SOX

State with the World's Largest
Indoor Waterfall

Michigan

The 114-foot (34.7-m) waterfall located in the lobby of the International Center in Detroit, Michigan, is the tallest indoor waterfall in the world. The backdrop of this impressive waterfall is a 9,000-square-foot (840-sq-m) slab of marble that was imported from the Greek island of Tinos and installed by eight marble craftsmen. About 6,000 gallons (27,276 l) of water spill down the waterfall each minute. That's the liquid equivalent of 80,000 cans of soda! Visitors can see this $1.5 million creation as they stroll through the International Center, which also houses many retail shops.

THE WORLD'S LARGEST
INDOOR WATERFALLS

Height in feet/meters

International Center, Michigan	Trump Tower, New York	Mohegan Sun, Connecticut	Orchid Hotel, India	Casino Windsor, Michigan
114 ft. 34.7 m.	90 ft. 27.4 m.	85 ft. 26.1 m.	70 ft. 21.3 m.	60 ft. 18.3 m.

State with the Largest
Hockey Stick

Minnesota

There is a hockey stick in the town of Eveleth, Minnesota, that measures 110 feet (33.5 m) long and weighs 5 tons (4.5 t). It was crafted in the exact same way a normal-size hockey stick would be, except the job called for about 3,000 times more wood. To transport the giant stick to Minnesota, the delivery truck had a state police escort to block some roads and intersections along the way. The giant hockey stick is positioned next to a 700-pound (318-kg) hockey puck. The stick was dedicated to the hockey players of the past, present, and future, and to the spirit of hockey in Eveleth.

THE UNITED STATES' LARGEST SPORTS EQUIPMENT MONUMENTS

Height in feet/meters

Hockey Stick, Minnesota	Baseball Bat, Kentucky	Bowling Pin, New Jersey	Arrows, Colorado	Soccer Ball, Missouri
110 ft. 33.5 m.	120 ft. 36.6 m.	24 ft. 7.3 m.	18 ft. 5.5 m.	12 ft. 3.6 m.

State with the
Most Catfish

Mississippi

There are more than 792 million catfish in Mississippi—more than 70% of the world's farm-raised supply. That's almost enough to give every person in the United States three fish each. The state's residents are quite proud of their successful fish industry. The World Catfish Festival is held every April in the town of Belzoni—also known as the Catfish Capital of the World. There, festival-goers can tour the Catfish Institute, which details the journey of the catfish from the pond to the plate.

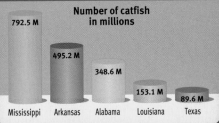

THE STATES WITH THE
MOST CATFISH

Number of catfish
in millions

Mississippi	Arkansas	Alabama	Louisiana	Texas
792.5 M	495.2 M	348.6 M	153.1 M	89.6 M

State with the Tallest Human-Made Monument

Missouri

The Gateway Arch in St. Louis towers 630 feet (192 m) above the ground. It is tall enough to be seen from up to 30 miles (48 km) away! A tram inside the arch carries people to an observation area at the top. On a busy day, some 5,500 people ride the arch's tram and get a spectacular view of the city. Built in 1965, this monument was first known as the Jefferson National Expansion Memorial. It was built to remind the world that St. Louis played an important part in the westward expansion of the United States.

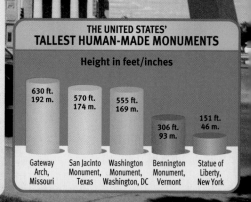

**THE UNITED STATES'
TALLEST HUMAN-MADE MONUMENTS**

Height in feet/inches

Monument	Height
Gateway Arch, Missouri	630 ft. / 192 m.
San Jacinto Monument, Texas	570 ft. / 174 m.
Washington Monument, Washington, DC	555 ft. / 169 m.
Bennington Monument, Vermont	306 ft. / 93 m.
Statue of Liberty, New York	151 ft. / 46 m.

State with the Oldest
National Monument

Montana

The Little Big Horn Battlefield National Monument, located near Crow Agency, Montana, was first designated a national cemetery in 1879. A memorial was built on Last Stand Hill two years later to commemorate the Seventh Cavalry soldiers who died there. The Battle of the Little Big Horn took place on June 25 and 26, 1876. General George Custer and the Seventh Calvary were defeated by the Lakota, Cheyenne, and Arapaho. Today, the memorial complex has a museum, hiking trails, and a research library.

THE UNITED STATES'
OLDEST NATIONAL MONUMENTS

Date established

Jan. 29, 1881	March 2, 1889	Sept. 24, 1906	Dec. 8, 1906	Dec. 8, 1906
Little Big Horn Battlefield, Montana	Casa Grande Ruins, Arizona	Devil's Tower, Wyoming	El Morro, New Mexico	Montezuma Castle, Arizona

State with the Most
Sandhill Cranes

Nebraska

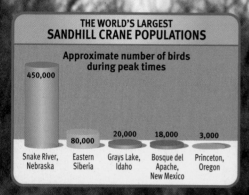

THE WORLD'S LARGEST
SANDHILL CRANE POPULATIONS

Approximate number of birds
during peak times

Snake River, Nebraska	450,000
Eastern Siberia	80,000
Grays Lake, Idaho	20,000
Bosque del Apache, New Mexico	18,000
Princeton, Oregon	3,000

For approximately five weeks each spring, Nebraska is the resting spot for 400,000 to 500,000 sandhill cranes. That's about 75% of the world's sandhill crane population! As part of their annual migration, these birds arrive from Texas, New Mexico, California, and Arizona to feed and rest along a 150-mile (241-km) stretch of the Platte River between Grand Isle and Sutherland. The Crane Meadows Nature Center is located along the Central Flyway and is a prime location to view and learn more about these cranes. The residents of this area celebrate the cranes' arrival during the annual Spring Wing Ding celebration.

State with the Largest
Glass Sculpture

Nevada

THE WORLD'S LARGEST
GLASS SCULPTURES

Length in feet/meters

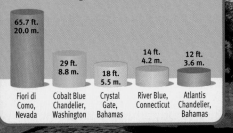

65.7 ft. 20.0 m.	29 ft. 8.8 m.	18 ft. 5.5 m.	14 ft. 4.2 m.	12 ft. 3.6 m.
Fiori di Como, Nevada	Cobalt Blue Chandelier, Washington	Crystal Gate, Bahamas	River Blue, Connecticut	Atlantis Chandelier, Bahamas

Fiori di Como—the breathtaking chandelier at the Bellagio Hotel in Las Vegas, Nevada—measures 65.6 feet by 29.5 feet (20 m by 9 m). Created by Dale Chihuly, the handblown glass chandelier consists of more than 2,000 discs of colored glass. Each disc is about 18 inches (45.7 cm) wide and hangs about 20 feet (6.1 m) overhead. Together, these colorful discs look like a giant field of flowers. The chandelier required about 10,000 pounds of steel (4,540 kg) and 40,000 pounds (18,160 kg) of handblown glass.

State with the Oldest
Covered Bridge

New Hampshire

The Haverhill-Bath Covered Bridge in New Hampshire was completed in 1832 and crosses the Ammonoosuc River to connect the towns of Haverhill and Bath. It has a two-lane span of 278 feet (85 m). Until 1999, the bridge had been open to cars and trucks. But because of its narrow width and the high cost of renovating the bridge, it is now only open to pedestrians and bicyclists. Today, New Hampshire has approximately 55 remaining covered bridges, but the number is shrinking due to deterioration from cold, harsh weather, vandalism, and neglect.

THE UNITED STATES'
OLDEST COVERED BRIDGES

Year built

Year built				
1832	1837	1840	1842	1845
Haverill-Bath Covered Bridge, New Hampshire	Cornwall Bridge, Connecticut	Coburn Bridge, Vermont	Perrine's Bridge, New York	Big Red Oak Creek Bridge, Georgia

State with the Largest
Toy Retailer Chain

New Jersey

Toys R Us—the world's largest toy retailer chain—has its headquarters in Paramus, New Jersey. The chain operates 1,597 stores, including more than 500 stores located in 27 foreign countries. Toys R Us averages annual sales of $11.8 billion and holds 15.6% of the market share in the United States. Some of the stores operated by the chain include Babies R Us, a store with infant clothing and furniture; Kids R Us, a clothing store for children; Imaginarium, a store specializing in learning and educational toys; and Geoffrey Stores, a store selling combination of all the products sold at Toys R Us chains.

THE COUNTRY'S LARGEST
TOY RETAILER CHAINS

Number of stores

Toys R Us	KB Toys	Hobby Lobby	Zany Brainy	Right Start
1,597	1,300	300	170	65

State with the World's Largest

Balloon Festival

New Mexico

Each October, approximately 1,000 hot air and gas-filled balloons take part in the Kodak Albuquerque International Balloon Fiesta in the skies over New Mexico. This event draws balloons from around the world, and is often seen in more than 50 countries. The festival takes place in the 350-acre (142-ha) Balloon Fiesta State Park. The Balloon Fiesta has also hosted some prestigious balloon races, including the Gordon Bennett Cup (1993), World Gas Balloon Championship (1994), and the America's Challenge Gas Balloon Race (1995).

THE WORLD'S LARGEST BALLOON FESTIVALS

Approximate number of balloons

Albuquerque, New Mexico	Gallup, New Mexico	Greenville, South Carolina	Gatineau, Canada	Reno, Nevada
1,000	200	150	150	125

State with the World's
Largest Cinema

New York

Radio City Music Hall in New York City is the world's largest cinema with 5,910 seats. Its marquee is a city block long, and the auditorium measures 84 feet (25.6 m) high—about half the height of the Statue of Liberty. The organ in the theater—known as the Mighty Wurlitzer—has pipes that reach up to 32 feet (9.7 m) high and are housed in eleven separate rooms. The theater opened in December 1932 and was originally known as The Showplace of the Nation. Since then, more than 300 million people have come to the Music Hall to see concerts, stage shows, movies, and special events. Radio City Music Hall has hosted more than 700 movie premieres, including *King Kong*, *Breakfast at Tiffany's*, *Mary Poppins*, and *The Lion King*.

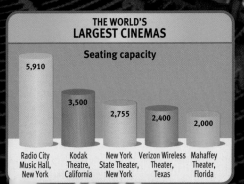

THE WORLD'S LARGEST CINEMAS

Seating capacity

5,910	3,500	2,755	2,400	2,000
Radio City Music Hall, New York	Kodak Theatre, California	New York State Theater, New York	Verizon Wireless Theater, Texas	Mahaffey Theater, Florida

State with the Oldest
State University

North Carolina

The University of North Carolina (UNC) was founded in 1789 but did not accept its first student at Chapel Hill until February 1795 because of a lack of funding. By the following month, the university consisted of 2 buildings, 2 professors, and 41 students. This makes UNC the only university in the United States to graduate students in the 18th century. Today, the University of North Carolina has more than 15,000 undergraduates and 2,400 faculty. The university has 16 campuses in the state, including Chapel Hill, Charlotte, Wilmington, and Asheville.

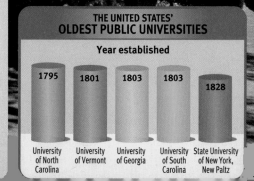

THE UNITED STATES'
OLDEST PUBLIC UNIVERSITIES

Year established

University of North Carolina	University of Vermont	University of Georgia	University of South Carolina	State University of New York, New Paltz
1795	1801	1803	1803	1828

State with the Largest
Hoofed Mammal

North Dakota

THE UNITED STATES' LARGEST HOOFED MAMMAL STATUES

Approximate size in feet/meters

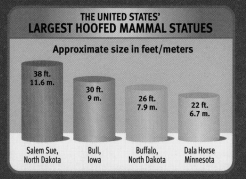

Salem Sue, North Dakota	Bull, Iowa	Buffalo, North Dakota	Dala Horse Minnesota
38 ft. 11.6 m.	30 ft. 9 m.	26 ft. 7.9 m.	22 ft. 6.7 m.

"Salem Sue" weighs about 12,000 pounds (5,443 kg) and stands 38 feet (11.6 m) above the fields that surround her. Salem Sue measures 50 feet (15m) long and is made out of fiberglass. The world's largest Holstein was built in 1974 and cost approximately $40,000. She was funded by area farmers, businesspeople, and local residents to celebrate New Salem's success in the dairy industry. The New Salem Lions organized the initial project and today continue to keep up Salem Sue's maintenance. Salem Sue also has a regional friend—North Dakota has the world's largest buffalo statue.

239

State with the Largest
Twins Gathering

Ohio

THE UNITED STATES'
LARGEST TWINS GATHERINGS

Number of attendees

Twins Day Festival, Ohio	International Twins Assoc. Annual Festival, Michigan	Annual Twins Gathering, New York	Nebraska Twins Convention, Nebraska	Michigan Twins Festival, Michigan
6,000	800	500	400	360

Each August, the town of Twinsburg, Ohio, hosts about 6,000 twins at its annual Twins Day Festival. Both identical and fraternal twins from around the world participate, and many dress alike. The twins take part in games, parades, and contests, such as the oldest identical twins and the twins with the widest combined smile. Since twins from ages 90 to just 11 days old have attended, there are special twin programs for all age groups. The event began in 1976 in honor of Aaron and Moses Wilcox, twin brothers who inspired the city to adopt its name in 1817.

State with the Largest
Military Museum

Oklahoma

Located in Oklahoma City, Oklahoma, the 45th Infantry Division Museum is spread over 12.5 acres (5 ha). Thousands of exhibits and artifacts related to the military history of Oklahoma are displayed in the museum's seven buildings. Some displays include exhibits that date back to 1541. Other galleries feature artifacts that take visitors through World War II and Desert Storm. The museum also features 200 of Bill Mauldin's original "Willie and Joe" cartoons about two riflemen in World War II, Korean-era artillery, original uniforms, and dioramas. The outdoor Military Park has more than 50 military vehicles, aircraft, and artillery.

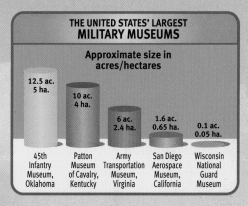

THE UNITED STATES' LARGEST
MILITARY MUSEUMS

Approximate size in acres/hectares

45th Infantry Museum, Oklahoma	12.5 ac. 5 ha.
Patton Museum of Cavalry, Kentucky	10 ac. 4 ha.
Army Transportation Museum, Virginia	6 ac. 2.4 ha.
San Diego Aerospace Museum, California	1.6 ac. 0.65 ha.
Wisconsin National Guard Museum	0.1 ac. 0.05 ha.

State with the World's
Longest Sea Cave

Oregon

Sea Lion Cave, located on the Pacific coast of Oregon, reaches a length of 360 feet (110 m). That's the same length as a football field. The cave is also 120 feet (37 m) from floor to ceiling. Sea Lion Cave began to form approximately 25 million years ago. One of the most amazing things about this natural wonder is its inhabitants. Two of the most common species of sea lions found in and around the caves include the Steller sea lion and the California sea lion. California gulls, western gulls, and herring gulls also live here. During the summer, gray whales can be seen feeding just offshore.

**THE WORLD'S
LONGEST SEA CAVES**

Length in feet/meters

360 ft. 110 m.	250 ft. 76 m.	230 ft. 70 m.	223 ft. 68 m.	200 ft. 61 m.
Sea Lion Cave, Oregon	Fingal's Cave, Scotland	Hamnsund-helleren, Norway	Smoo Cave, Scotland	Wookey Hole, England

State with the
Oldest Zoo

Pennsylvania

Although the Philadelphia Zoo was chartered in 1859, it didn't officially open its doors to the public until 1874 because of the Civil War. As the zoo grew, it continued to set records—it had the first adult male elephant ever exhibited in the United States (1888), the first orangutan birth in a U.S. zoo (1928), and the first zoo birth of cheetahs in the world (1956). Today, the Philadelphia Zoo cares for more than 1,600 animals from around the world. Some of its exhibits include the African Plains, the Amphibian and Reptile House, Bear Country, and Carnivore Kingdom. The large Animal Health Center is equipped to treat animals ranging from hummingbirds to polar bears.

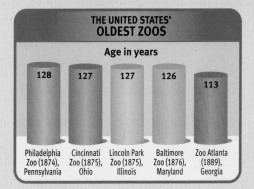

THE UNITED STATES'
OLDEST ZOOS

Age in years

Philadelphia Zoo (1874), Pennsylvania	Cincinnati Zoo (1875), Ohio	Lincoln Park Zoo (1875), Illinois	Baltimore Zoo (1876), Maryland	Zoo Atlanta (1889), Georgia
128	127	127	126	113

State with the
Oldest* Carousel

*Continually operating

Rhode Island

THE UNITED STATES' OLDEST
CONTINUALLY OPERATING CAROUSELS

Date built

1867	1884	1911	1912	1912
Flying Horse Carousel, Rhode Island	The Flying Horses, Massachusetts	Looff Carousel, California	The Grand Carousel, Pennsylvania	Trimper's Carousel, Maryland

The Flying Horse Carousel in Watch Hill, Rhode Island, was manufactured by the Charles W. Dare Company of New York in 1867. A traveling carnival was passing through the popular summer vacation spot and could no longer transport the carousel. The Flying Horse Carousel is unique because the horses are attached from chains on the ceiling, not poles from the floor. Each horse is hand-carved from a single piece of wood. The horses' tails and manes are made of real horsehair, and their saddles are made of leather.

State with the Oldest
Landscaped Gardens

South Carolina

The geometrical garden patterns in Middleton Place Gardens were designed by Henry Middleton in 1741 and were modeled after the gardens at the Palace of Versailles in France. They were first opened to the public in the 1920s. Today, the gardens on this 65-acre (26.3 ha) Charleston plantation are laid out in almost the same fashion as when they were planted more than 250 years ago. Some of the plants that are featured at Middleton Place Gardens include camellias, daffodils, magnolias, jasmine, columbine, and hydrangea.

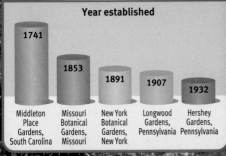

THE UNITED STATES' OLDEST LANDSCAPED GARDENS

Year established

1741	1853	1891	1907	1932
Middleton Place Gardens, South Carolina	Missouri Botanical Gardens, Missouri	New York Botanical Gardens, New York	Longwood Gardens, Pennsylvania	Hershey Gardens, Pennsylvania

State with the World's Largest Portrait Bust

South Dakota

THE WORLD'S LARGEST PORTRAIT BUSTS

Height in feet/meters

Mount Rushmore, South Dakota	Leshan Giant Buddha, China	Stone Mountain, Georgia	Statue of Liberty, New York	Lincoln Memorial, Washington, DC
500 ft. 152 m.	233 ft. 71 m.	200 ft. 61 m.	151 ft. 46 m.	19 ft. 6 m.

Located in the Black Hills of South Dakota, Mount Rushmore National Memorial features a 500-foot-high (152 m) portrait bust of four American presidents. The faces of George Washington, Thomas Jefferson, Abraham Lincoln, and Theodore Roosevelt are each about 60 feet (18.3 m) high. Gutzon Borglum began to carve this monument in 1927, but the work took 14 years to complete. The entire project cost only about $1 million. More than 2 million people visit the memorial each year.

State with the World's Largest Freshwater Aquarium

Tennessee

THE WORLD'S LARGEST FRESHWATER AQUARIUMS

Size in square feet/ square meters

Tennessee Aquarium, Tennessee, USA	The Freshwater Center, Denmark	Great Lakes Aquarium, Minnesota, USA	Aquarium of the Lakes, Britain	Belle Isle Aquarium, Michigan, USA
130,000 sq. ft. 12,077 sq. m.	91,494 sq. ft. 8,500 sq. m.	62,000 sq. ft. 5,760 sq. m.	49,514 sq. ft. 4,600 sq. m.	28,000 sq. ft. 2,601 sq. m.

The Tennessee Aquarium in Chattanooga is an impressive 130,000 square feet (12,077 sq m), making it the largest freshwater aquarium in the world. An additional 60,000-square-foot (5,574-sq-m) area will open in spring 2005. Permanent features in the aquarium include an IMAX theater, Discovery Hall, and an Environmental Learning Lab. Some of the aquarium's 9,000 animals include baby alligators, paddlefish, lake sturgeon, seadragons, and pipefish. And to feed all of these creatures, the aquarium goes through 12,000 crickets, 33,300 worms, and 1,200 pounds (545 kg) of seafood each month!

247

State with the Biggest
Ferris Wheel

Texas

The State Fair of Texas boasts the nation's largest ferris wheel. Called the Texas Star, this colossal wheel measures 212 feet (64.6 m) high. That's taller than a 20-story building! The Texas Star was built in Italy and shipped to Texas for its debut at the 1986 fair. The Texas Star is just one of the 70 rides featured at the fair. The three-week-long State Fair of Texas is held in the fall, and the giant ferris wheel is not the only grand-scale item there. Big Tex, a 52-foot- (15.9-m) tall cowboy, is the fair's mascot and the biggest cowboy in the United States.

THE UNITED STATES' LARGEST FERRIS WHEELS

Height of wheel in feet/meters

Texas Star, Texas	Colossus, Massachusetts	Giant Wheel, Ohio	Navy Pier Ferris Wheel, Illinois	Six Flags Ferris Wheel, Kentucky
212 ft. 64.6 m.	150 ft. 45.8 m.	150 ft. 45.8 m.	150 ft. 45.8 m.	150 ft. 45.8 m.

State with the World's Largest Corn Maze

Utah

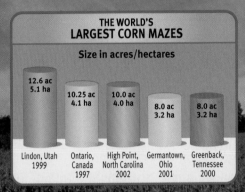

THE WORLD'S LARGEST CORN MAZES

Size in acres/hectares

12.6 ac 5.1 ha	10.25 ac 4.1 ha	10.0 ac 4.0 ha	8.0 ac 3.2 ha	8.0 ac 3.2 ha
Lindon, Utah 1999	Ontario, Canada 1997	High Point, North Carolina 2002	Germantown, Ohio 2001	Greenback, Tennessee 2000

In June 1999, Brett Herbst created a giant cornfield maze in Lindon, Utah, that covered 12.6 acres (5.1 ha) and had paths that measured 7.5 feet (2.3 m) wide. Herbst, a Brigham Young University graduate who majored in agriculture, constructed his first maze in 1996 and drew 18,000 visitors in less than 3 weeks. With such success, he decided to form his own company—called The MAIZE—that plans and constructs cornfield mazes. Since forming the company Herbst has produced more than 330 mazes that about 2 million visitors have enjoyed. It takes between 30 minutes and 3 hours to exit one of the corn mazes.

State That Produces the
Most Maple Syrup

Vermont

Maple syrup production in Vermont totaled 495,000 gallons (1,874,000 l) in 2002 and accounted for about 37% of the United States' total crop that year. There are about 2,000 maple syrup producers in Vermont, and the annual production totals more than $13 million. It takes about 5 tree taps to produce enough maple sap—approximately 40 gallons (150 l)—to produce just 1 gallon (3.79 l) of syrup. Vermont maple syrup is also made into maple sugar, maple cream, and maple candies.

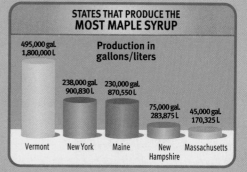

STATES THAT PRODUCE THE MOST MAPLE SYRUP

495,000 gal. 1,800,000 L — **Production in gallons/liters**

Vermont	New York	Maine	New Hampshire	Massachusetts
495,000 gal. 1,800,000 L	238,000 gal. 900,830 L	230,000 gal. 870,550 L	75,000 gal. 283,875 L	45,000 gal. 170,325 L

Birthplace of the
Most Presidents

Virginia

The Commonwealth of Virginia has earned the nickname "the Mother of Presidents" because eight of America's chief executives were born there. These presidents are George Washington (1st; 1789–1797), Thomas Jefferson (3rd; 1801–1809), James Madison (4th; 1809–1817), James Monroe (5th; 1817–1825), William Henry Harrison (9th; 1841), John Tyler (10th; 1841–1845), Zachary Taylor (12th; 1849–1850), and Woodrow Wilson (28th; 1913–1921). Since the first colony was founded here in 1607, Virginia has played a big part in the nation's political development. Each year many tourists visit Virginia's historical sites to learn more about the country's past.

BIRTHPLACES OF THE MOST PRESIDENTS

Virginia	Ohio	Massachusetts	New York	Texas
8	7	4	4	3

Mount Vernon, former home of President George Washington

State That Produces the
Most Apples

Washington

The state of Washington produces about 5.7 billion pounds (2.6 billion kg) of apples in just one year. That's enough to give every person in the world 18 pounds (8 kg) of apples annually. The Columbia Basin is where most of the state's produce is grown. Located in the central part of Washington, its fertile, well-drained soil is ideal for apple trees. In the United States, about one-half of the annual apple crop is sold as fresh fruit. Another one-fifth of the apple crop is used for juice, jelly, apple butter, and vinegar.

THE UNITED STATES'
TOP APPLE-PRODUCING STATES

Apples produced, in billions and millions of pounds/kilograms

Washington	New York	Michigan	California	Pennsylvania
5.7 B lbs. 2.6 B kg.	996 M lbs. 452 M kg.	852 M lbs. 387 M kg.	646 M lbs. 293 M kg.	474 M lbs. 215 M kg.

State with the World's Longest Steel Arch Bridge

West Virginia

THE WORLD'S LONGEST STEEL ARCH BRIDGES

Length of main span in feet/meters

New River Gorge Bridge, West Virginia, USA	Bayonne Bridge, New Jersey, USA	Sydney Harbor Bridge, Australia	Zdakov Bridge, Czech Republic	Port Mann Bridge, Canada
1,700 ft. 518 m.	1,675 ft. 511 m.	1,670 ft. 509 m.	1,244 ft. 379 m.	1,200 ft. 366 m.

With a main span of 1,700 feet (518 m) and a weight of about 88 million pounds (40 million kg), the New River Gorge Bridge in Fayetteville, West Virginia, is the longest and largest steel arch bridge in the world. It is approximately 875 feet (267 m) above the New River and is the second highest bridge in the United States. After three years of construction, the bridge was completed in 1977. This $37-million structure is the focus of Bridge Day—a statewide annual festival that commemorates its building. This is the only day that the New River Gorge Bridge is open to pedestrians.

State with North America's Longest
Cross-Country Ski Race

Wisconsin

The American Birkebeiner cross-country ski marathon is the longest cross-country ski race in North America. The trail winds for 31.7 miles (51 km) through the woods of northern Wisconsin and finishes on Main Street in Hayward. Since it began in 1973, skiers from all parts of the world take part in this event each February. The "Birke" is part of the Worldloppet circuit of 14 international ski marathons and is also part of the International Ski Federation Marathon Cup Series. On race day, skiers and spectators consume approximately 10,000 oranges, 4,000 cups of hot chocolate, 5,000 gallons of water, and 16,000 cookies.

**NORTH AMERICA'S
LONGEST CROSS-COUNTRY SKI RACES**

Length of race in miles/kilometers

31.7 mi. 51 km.	31.0 mi. 50 km.	27.0 mi. 44 km.	18.6 mi. 30 km.	13.0 mi. 21 km.
American Birkebeiner, Wisconsin	North America Vasa Cross-Country Race, Michigan	Governor's Cup, Minnesota	Boulder Mountain Tour, Idaho	North End Classic, Wisconsin

State with the Oldest
National Park

Wyoming

The U.S. Congress designated the Yellowstone region of eastern Wyoming as the world's first national park in March 1872. Many geological features found at Yellowstone are unusual. In fact, the park has more than 10,000 hot springs and 200 geysers—the greatest concentration of geothermal features in the world. Yellowstone is also known for its wildlife. Bison, bighorn sheep, moose, black bears, wolves, and many species of birds and fish can be found in the park. This giant preserve covers almost 3,470 square miles (8,987 sq km) of mostly undeveloped land.

THE UNITED STATES' OLDEST NATIONAL PARKS

Year founded

1872	1890	1890	1890	1899
Yellowstone, Wyoming, Montana, Idaho	Sequoia, California	Kings Canyon, California	Yosemite, California	Mt. Rainier, Washington

Human-Made Records

Constructions • Travel • Transportation

World's Highest
Suspension Bridge

Royal Gorge

THE WORLD'S
HIGHEST SUSPENSION BRIDGES

Height in feet/meters

1,053 ft.
321 m.

318 ft.
97 m.

228 ft.
69 m.

220 ft.
67 m.

203 ft.
62 m.

Royal Gorge, USA • Akashi Kaiyo, Japan • Verrazano-Narrows, USA • Golden Gate, USA • Tsing Ma, China

The Royal Gorge Bridge—in Canon City, Colorado—spans the Arkansas River 1,053 feet (321 m) above the water. The bridge is 1,260 feet (384 m) long and 18 feet (5 m) wide. About 1,000 tons (907 t) of steel make up the bridge's floor, which can hold in excess of 2 million pounds (907,200 kg). The cables weigh about 300 tons (272 t) each. The bridge took just five months to complete in 1929 at a cost of $350,000.

World's Longest
Suspension Bridge

Akashi-Kaikyo

This giant suspension bridge connects Maiko, Tarumi Ward, in Kobe City to Matsuho, Awaji Town. All together, the bridge spans the Akashi Strait for 2 miles (3219 m) in Tsuna County on the Japanese island of Awajishima. Built in 1998, the structure's main span is a record-breaking 6,529 feet (1,990 m) long with cables supporting the 100,000 ton (90,700 t) bridge below. Each cable is made up of 290 strands of wire. More than 186,000 miles (30,000 km) of wire was used for the project—enough to circle Earth 7.5 times!

The main tower soars approximately 984 feet (300 m) into the air.

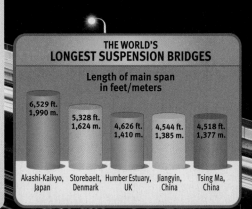

THE WORLD'S LONGEST SUSPENSION BRIDGES

Length of main span in feet/meters

Akashi-Kaikyo, Japan	6,529 ft. 1,990 m.
Storebaelt, Denmark	5,328 ft. 1,624 m.
Humber Estuary, UK	4,626 ft. 1,410 m.
Jiangyin, China	4,544 ft. 1,385 m.
Tsing Ma, China	4,518 ft. 1,377 m.

World's Tallest Hotel

Burj Al Arab

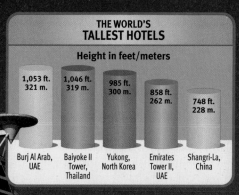

THE WORLD'S TALLEST HOTELS

Height in feet/meters

Burj Al Arab, UAE	Baiyoke II Tower, Thailand	Yukong, North Korea	Emirates Tower II, UAE	Shangri-La, China
1,053 ft. 321 m.	1,046 ft. 319 m.	985 ft. 300 m.	858 ft. 262 m.	748 ft. 228 m.

The Burj Al Arab—or Tower of the Arabs—in Dubai, United Arab Emirates (UAE) towers an incredible 1,053 feet (321 m) above the ground. This makes it the world's tallest hotel, as well as the sixteenth-tallest building in the world. The hotel is shaped like a ship's billowing sail and is a part of the Jumeirah Beach resort. It was built in 1999 on a human-made island in the Arabian Gulf. Guests at the Burj Al Arab can enjoy 202 luxury suites. Kids staying at the hotel will enjoy the family pool with a beach and rock wall waterslide. Rooms in this amazing hotel start at around $1,000 per night.

World's Tallest
Habitable Building

Petronas Towers

THE WORLD'S
TALLEST HABITABLE BUILDINGS

Height in feet/meters

1,483 ft. 452 m.	1,454 ft. 443 m.	1,381 ft. 421 m.	1,352 ft. 412 m.	1,283 ft. 391 m.
Petronas Twin Towers, Malaysia	Sears Tower, USA	Jin Mao Building, China	Two International Finance Center, China	CITIC Plaza, China

Each of these giant, identical skyscrapers is 1,483 feet (452 m) tall. They soar above the city of Kuala Lumpur in Malaysia and contain the headquarters for Petronas, the country's national petroleum company. The two 88-story towers are circular, with a 191-foot- (58-m) long sky bridge that connects them at the forty-first and forty-second floors. By elevator, it takes just 90 seconds to travel from the basement floor to the top of each tower. Together, the towers have 32,000 windows, taking window washers two months to completely wash both buildings. These giant buildings were created by American architect Cesar Pelli and completed in 1998 at a cost of $1.6 billion.

City with the Most
Skyscrapers

New York City

New York City has 164 skyscrapers towering over its streets. At the mouth of the Hudson River in southeastern New York State, New York City is an area of more than 308 square miles (797 sq km). A solid platform of bedrock has made it possible for the island to support such large structures. Some of the city's tallest skyscrapers—such as the Empire State Building and the Chrysler Building—are world famous. Skyscrapers first became popular in New York in the 1870s, when real estate prices in Manhattan made it more economical to build up instead of out.

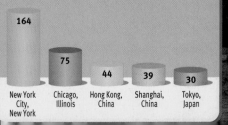

WORLD CITIES WITH THE MOST SKYSCRAPERS

Number of skyscrapers

City	Number
New York City, New York	164
Chicago, Illinois	75
Hong Kong, China	44
Shanghai, China	39
Tokyo, Japan	30

World's Tallest
Apartment Building

Trump World Tower

Trump World Tower in New York City rises 863 feet (263 m) above Manhattan, making it the world's tallest apartment building. Located in the United Nations Plaza and built by billionaire Donald Trump, this 72-story engineering marvel offers truly luxurious condominiums. Some amenities include a private spa and health club, a world-class restaurant, a 60-foot (18.3-m) swimming pool, and a landscaped garden. Condos feature marble bathrooms, maple hardwood floors, 16-foot (4.8-m) ceilings, and state-of-the-art appliances. These spectacular homes range from $1.0 to $13.5 million.

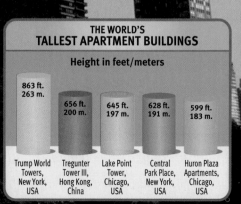

THE WORLD'S TALLEST APARTMENT BUILDINGS

Height in feet/meters

Height	Building
863 ft. 263 m.	Trump World Towers, New York, USA
656 ft. 200 m.	Tregunter Tower III, Hong Kong, China
645 ft. 197 m.	Lake Point Tower, Chicago, USA
628 ft. 191 m.	Central Park Place, New York, USA
599 ft. 183 m.	Huron Plaza Apartments, Chicago, USA

World's
Largest Mall

West Edmonton Mall

The West Edmonton Mall—located in Alberta, Canada—occupies a total of 5.3 million square feet (.47 million sq m). This giant shopping and entertainment complex features more than 800 stores and restaurants. In addition to stores and eateries, the West Edmonton Mall also houses the world's largest indoor amusement park, the world's largest indoor lake with four working submarines, World Waterpark with the world's largest wave pool, Sea Life Caverns, an NHL-size ice arena, 26 movie theaters, dolphin shows, a casino, and a miniature golf course.

THE WORLD'S LARGEST MALLS

Area in millions of square feet/square meters

5.3 M sq. ft. 0.47 M sq. m.	4.2 M sq. ft. 0.39 M sq. m.	3.0 M sq. ft. 0.27 M sq. m.	2.3 M sq. ft. 0.21 M sq. m.	0.9 M sq. ft. 0.08 M sq. m.
West Edmonton Mall, Canada	Mall of America, Minnesota, USA	Del Amo Fashion Center, California, USA	Woodfield Mall, Illinois, USA	Sunter City Mall, Singapore

Amusement Park with the Most Rides

Cedar Point

Cedar Point in Sandusky, Ohio, has 68 rides for park goers to enjoy. The tallest, The Space Spiral, reaches 330 feet (100 m) into the sky and gives riders an amazing view. Another tall ride—the 300-foot (91-m) Power Tower—blasts riders up and down the towers at speeds of 55 miles (89 km) per hour. And with fifteen roller coasters, Cedar Point also has the most coasters of any theme park in the world. More than 44,500 feet (13,572 m) of coaster track—more than 6 miles (9.6 km)—run through the park. Cedar Point opened in 1870 and is the second-oldest amusement park in the country.

THE AMUSEMENT PARKS WITH THE MOST RIDES

Number of rides

Cedar Point, Ohio	Hershey Park, Pennsylvania	Disneyland, California	Legoland, California	Magic Kingdom, Florida
68	59	45	40	24

World's
Highest City

Wenchuan, China

Wenchuan, China, sits 16,730 feet (5,103 m) above the sea. That's 3.2 miles (5.2 km) high, more than half the height of Mt. Everest. There are several ancient villages in the area with houses dating back hundreds of years. Located nearby is the Wolong Panda Preserve—one of the last places on Earth where the endangered bears are studied and bred. The city is part of the Sichuan Province, which is located in southwest China. The province covers 207,340 square miles (537,000 sq km) and has a population of 94.5 million.

THE WORLD'S
HIGHEST CITIES

Height above sea level
in feet/meters

Wenchuan, China	Potosi, Bolivia	Oruro, Bolivia	Lhasa, Tibet	La Paz, Bolivia
16,730 ft. 5,099 m.	13,045 ft. 3,976 m.	12,146 ft. 3,702 m.	12,087 ft. 3,684 m.	11,916 ft. 3,632 m.

World's Most
Massive Dam

Tarbela Dam

The Tarbela Dam on the Indus River in Pakistan can hold an amazing 5,244 million cubic feet (148.5 million cu m) of water. The dam measures 469 feet (143 m) high and 2,264 feet (691 m) thick at the base. The dam was built in 1976 by more than 15,000 workers and engineers at a cost of $900 million. Although the dam was originally built to store water for agricultural purposes, the release of water also produces electricity.

THE WORLD'S MOST MASSIVE DAMS

Volume in millions of cubic feet/meters

Tarbela, Pakistan	Fort Peck, USA	Tucurui, Brazil	Ataturk, Turkey	Yacireta, Argentina
5,244 M cu. ft. 148.5 M cu. m.	3,390 M cu. ft. 96.0 M cu. m.	3,009 M cu. ft. 85.2 M cu. m.	3,002 M cu. ft. 85.0 M cu. m.	2,861 cu. ft. 81.0 M cu. m.

World's Longest
Underwater Tunnel

Seikan Tunnel

The Seikan Tunnel stretches underwater for a total of 33.4 miles (53.8 km), making it both the longest railway tunnel and underwater tunnel in the world. It connects Honshu—the main island of Japan—to Hokkaido, an island to the north. Some 14.3 miles (23 km) of the tunnel run under the Tsugaru Strait, which connects the Pacific Ocean to the Sea of Japan. A railway in the tunnel transports passengers. Construction began in 1964 and took 24 years to complete. Today, the Seikan Tunnel is no longer the quickest way between the two islands. Air travel is faster and almost the same price.

**THE WORLD'S
LONGEST UNDERWATER TUNNELS**

Length in miles/kilometers

Tunnel	Length
Seikan Tunnel, Japan	33.4 mi. 53.6 km.
Channel Tunnel, France/England	31.0 mi. 49.9 km.
Dai-Shimizu Tunnel, Japan	13.8 mi. 22.2 km.
Shin-Kanmo Tunnel, Japan	11.6 mi. 18.8 km.
Tokyo Bay Aqualine, Japan	5.0 mi. 9.5 km.

World's Longest Road Tunnel

Laerdal

The 15.2-mile (24.5-km) Laerdal Tunnel was officially opened in Norway on November 27, 2000. This huge construction makes its way under large mountain chains to connect the capital of Oslo to the port of Bergen, Norway's second-largest city. The tunnel is 29.5 feet (9 m) wide and 21 feet (6.3 m) high. It is estimated that about 1,000 cars and trucks make the 20-minute drive through the tunnel each day. To help make the tunnel safe, the designers installed fire extinguishers every 410 feet (125 m) and special lighting to keep drivers alert. There are also many parking spaces and turning areas in case drivers need to stop or have car trouble. The Laerdal Tunnel cost about $114 million to build.

268

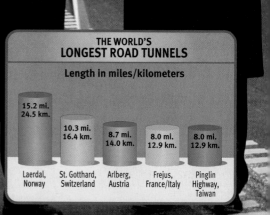

THE WORLD'S LONGEST ROAD TUNNELS

Length in miles/kilometers

15.2 mi. 24.5 km.	10.3 mi. 16.4 km.	8.7 mi. 14.0 km.	8.0 mi. 12.9 km.	8.0 mi. 12.9 km.
Laerdal, Norway	St. Gotthard, Switzerland	Arlberg, Austria	Frejus, France/Italy	Pinglin Highway, Taiwan

Most-Visited National Park

Great Smoky Mountains

Each year about 9.2 million people travel to North Carolina and Tennessee to visit the Great Smoky Mountains. The national park is 800 square miles (2,072 sq km), of which about 95% is forested. While at the park, visitors can admire some of the area's many waterfalls while enjoying some 850 miles (1,368 km) of hiking trails and 550 miles (885 km) of horseback riding trails. Visitors may also see some of the park's 4,130 different plant and tree species or 300 bird and animal species.

GREAT SMOKY MOUNTAINS NATIONAL PARK

AN INTERNATIONAL BIOSPHERE RESERVE

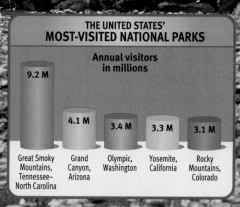

THE UNITED STATES' MOST-VISITED NATIONAL PARKS

Annual visitors in millions

Great Smoky Mountains, Tennessee–North Carolina	Grand Canyon, Arizona	Olympic, Washington	Yosemite, California	Rocky Mountains, Colorado
9.2 M	4.1 M	3.4 M	3.3 M	3.1 M

269

World's
Busiest Airport

Hartsfield Atlanta Airport

In one year, an average of more than 75 million passengers travel through the Hartsfield Atlanta International Airport. That's more people than are living in California, Texas, and Florida combined. Approximately 2,346 planes depart and arrive at this airport every day. With parking lots, runways, maintenance facilities, and other buildings, the Hartsfield terminal complex covers about 130 acres (53 ha). Hartsfield Atlanta Airport has a north and south terminal, as well as an underground train and six concourses that feature many shops, restaurants, and banks.

THE WORLD'S BUSIEST AIRPORTS

Annual passengers in millions

Hartsfield Atlanta Intl., USA	Chicago O'Hare Intl., USA	Los Angeles Intl., USA	Heathrow Intl., England	Haneda Intl., Japan
75.8 M	66.8 M	61.0 M	60.7 M	58.7 M

Country with the
Most Airports

The United States

The United States leads the world with 14,695 airports. That is more than the number of airports for the other nine top countries combined. The top three busiest airports in the world are also located in the United States. All together, U.S. airports serve more than 608 million travelers a year. However, with the threat of terrorism and the state of the economy, the airline industry lost $10 billion in 2002. Today several of the country's largest airlines are close to bankruptcy.

THE COUNTRIES WITH THE MOST AIRPORTS

Number of airports

USA	Brazil	Russia	Mexico	Argentina
14,695	3,365	2,743	1,852	1,369

World's Top
Tourist Country

France

Each year, more than 76 million tourists visit France. That's equal to the number of people living in all of California, Florida, and Texas combined. The most popular French destinations are Paris and the Mediterranean coast. In July and August—the most popular time to visit France—tourists flock to the westernmost coastal areas of the region. In the winter, visitors hit the slopes at some major ski resorts in the northern Alps. Tourists also visit many of France's world-renowned landmarks and monuments, including the Eiffel Tower, Notre Dame, the Louvre, and the Arc de Triomphe. Most tourists are from other European countries, especially Germany.

THE WORLD'S TOP TOURIST COUNTRIES

International visitors in millions

France	Spain	USA	Italy	China
76.5 M	49.5 M	45.5 M	39.0 M	33.2 M

World's Most-Visited Amusement Park

Tokyo Disneyland

In 2002, more than 17 million people visited Japan's Tokyo Disneyland. Adventureland features landscapes from around the world, while World Bazaar and Westernland focus on nineteenth-century America. Tomorrowland helps visitors explore the galaxy and learn about future technology. The park's Fantasyland is home to Cinderella Castle, but most of the other Disney characters live in Toontown.

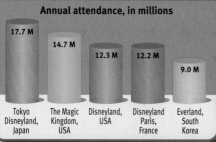

THE WORLD'S MOST-VISITED THEME PARKS

Annual attendance, in millions

Park	Attendance
Tokyo Disneyland, Japan	17.7 M
The Magic Kingdom, USA	14.7 M
Disneyland, USA	12.3 M
Disneyland Paris, France	12.2 M
Everland, South Korea	9.0 M

Country with the Most
Bicycles per Capita

The Netherlands

With an estimated 16.5 million bicycles in the country, the Netherlands has more bicycles per capita than any other nation. It averages out to about one bike for every person in the country. Many people around the world—especially those in crowded cities—have realized that bicycling is an easy way to get around and a great way to cut down on pollution. The Netherlands, in particular, is battling a major pollution problem, and it is one of the world's most densely populated nations.

COUNTRIES WITH THE HIGHEST PER CAPITA BIKE OWNERSHIP

Bikes per person

Netherlands	Germany	Japan	USA	China
1.00	0.89	0.55	0.44	0.41

Country with the
Most Cars

The United States

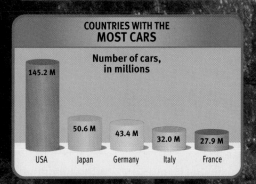

COUNTRIES WITH THE MOST CARS

Number of cars, in millions

USA	Japan	Germany	Italy	France
145.2 M	50.6 M	43.4 M	32.0 M	27.9 M

The citizens of the United States own 145.2 million automobiles. That's about 31% of all the automobiles owned in the world. It means that for every two Americans there is one car. That figure doesn't even include all of the trucks, campers, and motorcycles in the country. Almost 90% of all U.S. residents have access to motor vehicles. With 17.8 million cars, California is the state with the most registered automobiles in the nation. Each year, U.S. drivers total about 4.3 trillion passenger miles (6.9 million passenger km) of travel and burn about 200 billion gallons (757 billion liters) of fuel. Americans also spend about 38 hours each year stuck in traffic.

Country with the Most Roads

United States

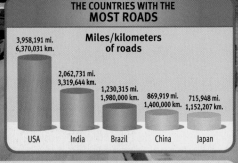

THE COUNTRIES WITH THE MOST ROADS

Miles/kilometers of roads

3,958,191 mi. 6,370,031 km.	2,062,731 mi. 3,319,644 km.	1,230,315 mi. 1,980,000 km.	869,919 mi. 1,400,000 km.	715,948 mi. 1,152,207 km.
USA	India	Brazil	China	Japan

There are 3,958,191 miles (6,370,031 km) of roads that crisscross the United States. Approximately 5.7 million miles (3.5 million km) of these roads are paved. About three-quarters of the roads, or 2.9 million miles (1.8 million km), are part of the national road system. Each person in America makes an average of four outings and travels some 39 miles (24 km) each day. Because Americans are always on the move, it's not surprising that the nation's highways are frequently tied up with traffic jams. People waste about 7 billion gallons (31.8 billion l) of fuel and 4.3 billion hours annually because they are stuck in traffic.

City with the Busiest Subway System

Moscow

THE WORLD'S BUSIEST SUBWAY SYSTEMS

Passengers per year in billions

- Moscow: 3.28 B
- Tokyo: 2.92 B
- Seoul: 1.61 B
- Mexico City: 1.30 B
- New York City: 1.14 B

Each year, approximately 3.28 billion people ride on Moscow's bustling Metropolitan (Metro) subway system. It is not only busy, it is also world renowned for its beautiful architecture. Many of the 150 stations have stained glass, marble statuary, and sparkling chandeliers. The rail network is 153 miles (246 km) long and follows the street pattern above. About half of the subway riders travel for free because they are either students, retirees, police officers, or military personnel. Other riders pay 4 rubles, or about 14 cents, per ride.

Money and
Business Records

Most Valuable • Industry • Wealth

World's Most Expensive
Pop Memorabilia

John Lennon's Phantom V Rolls-Royce

Jim Pattison with John Lennon's Phantom V Rolls-Royce

THE WORLD'S MOST VALUABLE POP MEMORABILIA

Cost at auction

Item	Cost
John Lennon's Phantom V Rolls-Royce	$2.29 M
John Lennon's Steinway Model Z Piano	$2.15 M
Eric Clapton's Guitar "Brownie"	$491,500
Bernie Taupin's revised "Candle in the Wind" lyrics	$400,000
Jimi Hendrix's Fender Stratocaster Guitar	$370,260

At a Sotheby's auction in 1983, Jim Pattison's company—Ripley International Inc.—bought John Lennon's Phantom V Rolls-Royce touring limousine for $2.29 million. Lennon, of the group The Beatles, bought the car in 1965. Quickly bored with the plain black exterior, Lennon had the car painted psychedelic colors and designs. In 1970, Lennon had the Phantom V shipped to the United States and loaned it to several rock stars, including the Rolling Stones, the Moody Blues, and Bob Dylan.

279

World's Most
Valuable Barbie®

40th Anniversary De Beers

**THE WORLD'S
MOST VALUABLE BARBIE® DOLLS**

Price in US dollars

$82,870	$17,000	$9,500	$7,500	$7,000
De Beers	Original Prototype	1959 Ponytail #1, Brunette	1959 Ponytail #1, Blonde	1959 Ponytail #2, Brunette

To celebrate the fortieth anniversary of Barbie®in 1999, the De Beers diamond company helped to create a customized doll worth $82,870. This Barbie® is adorned with 160 diamonds, which weigh almost 20 carats, and are set in 18-karat white gold. One fastener on the dress can be removed and worn as a brooch. Even after 40 years in production, much attention is paid to the regular Barbie® doll's clothes. To date, about 59,000 miles (94,990 km) of fabric has been used to create her fashions, including designs from Vera Wang, Christian Dior, and Bob Mackie.

World's Most Valuable Teddy Bear

Louis Vuitton Steiff Bear

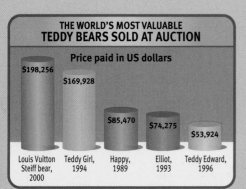

THE WORLD'S MOST VALUABLE TEDDY BEARS SOLD AT AUCTION

Price paid in US dollars

$198,256	Louis Vuitton Steiff bear, 2000
$169,928	Teddy Girl, 1994
$85,470	Happy, 1989
$74,275	Elliot, 1993
$53,924	Teddy Edward, 1996

In October 2000, a Steiff teddy bear dressed in Louis Vuitton clothes fetched an amazing $198,256 at the Teddies de l'An 2000 auction in Monaco. The 17-inch-tall (43-cm-tall) bear has jointed arms and legs and is made of the finest mohair. It is signed by the president of Steiff and has a special edition ear tag. The Monaco Aide et Presence—the charity that benefited from the auction—and the year 2000 are embroidered on its left foot. Industrialist Jesse Kim bought the bear for his new museum. He hopes to encourage teddy bear collecting in Korea.

Most Expensive
Movie Memorabilia

Best Film Oscar® for *Gone With the Wind*

David Selznick receiving the Oscar® for Gone With the Wind.

David Selznick's Best Film Oscar® for producing the film classic *Gone With the Wind* was purchased by pop superstar Michael Jackson for $1.54 million. Jackson's agent called Sotheby's in June 1999 and entered into a bidding war for the coveted award. Eventually, the Oscar® went to Jackson for a price that was more than five times higher than its estimated value of $300,000. Jackson said it was his lifelong dream to own the Oscar®. Memorabilia from *Gone With the Wind*—the 1939 film starring Vivien Leigh and Clark Gable—has long been especially popular and often fetches a high price on the auction block.

282

THE WORLD'S MOST EXPENSIVE MOVIE MEMORABILIA SOLD AT AUCTION

Price paid in US dollars

$1,540,000				
	$666,000	$562,500	$507,500	$453,500
David Selznick's *Gone With the Wind* Oscar®	Judy Garland's Ruby Slippers	Vivien Leigh's *Gone With the Wind* Oscar®	Clark Gable's *It Happened One Night* Oscar®	Poster for *The Mummy*, 1932

World's Most Expensive Jewels at Auction

Jadeite Necklace

These jadeite gems are similar to those used in the jadeite necklace.

THE WORLD'S MOST VALUABLE JEWELS

Price at auction in millions of US dollars

Jewel	Price
Jadeite Necklace	$9.39 M
The Begum Blue Diamond	$7.79 M
Mouna Diamond Brooch	$3.23 M
Allnat Pendant	$3.04 M
Harcourt Emeralds	$2.87 M

On November 6, 1997, a private collector placed a telephone bid of $9.39 million for a jadeite necklace that was being auctioned by Christie's in Hong Kong. The necklace was made of 27 beads, which means each tiny jadeite bead cost about $347,778! Jadeite is a mineral that is made up mostly of sodium and aluminum. It is considered one of the most precious stones in China and Japan, and many artists have carved beautiful works of art from jadeite. Many of these carvings, including vases, jewels, bowls, and statues, are

World's Most Valuable
Baseball

Mark McGwire's 70th Home Run Baseball

Businessman and baseball fan Todd McFarlane made sports history himself when he paid $3.05 million for Mark McGwire's 70th home run baseball in January 1999. The bid, which was actually $2.7 million plus a large commission fee, is the most money paid for a sports artifact. The ball was only expected to sell for about $1 million. McFarlane said he bought the ball because he wanted to own a piece of history. This famous baseball marked the end of the exciting 1998 home run race between Mark McGwire and Sammy Sosa. Both beat Roger Maris's three-decade record of 61. Sosa with 66 and McGwire with 70.

THE WORLD'S MOST VALUABLE BASEBALLS

Price paid at auction, in US dollars

$3.05 M	McGwire's 70th Home Run Baseball
$517,500	Bonds' 73rd Home Run Baseball
$150,000	Sosa's 66th Home Run Baseball
$125,500	Ruth's First Yankee Stadium Home Run Baseball
$60,000	Baseball Autographed by Ruth and Maris

World's Most Valuable
Food Brand

Coca-Cola

Coca-Cola is the most valuable food brand in the world, worth some $72.5 billion. Coca-Cola was invented in the United States by John Pemberton in 1887. He quickly trademarked his mix of Coca-Cola syrup and carbonated water and it became a popular fountain drink. Today about 300 different Coca-Cola products can be found in 200 countries around the globe. Most well-known brands like Coke and Sprite are widely available, but some countries have their own special flavors. For instance, Brazilians enjoy Bonaqua, the Japanese drink Sokebicha, and Israelis may quench their thirst with Kinley.

THE WORLD'S MOST VALUABLE FOOD BRANDS

Worth in billions of US dollars

Coca-Cola	McDonald's	Nescafé	Heinz	Budweiser
$72.5 B	$27.8 B	$13.6 B	$11.7 B	$10.7 B

285

Country That Spends the Most on Toys

United States

COUNTRIES THAT
SPEND THE MOST ON TOYS

Billions of dollars spent

USA	Japan	UK	France	Germany
$34.5 B	$9.1 B	$5.3 B	$3.3 B	$3.1 B

Each year Americans spend an amazing $34.5 billion on toys! That means that every single person in the country spends an average of $121 on toys annually. That's not too much of a surprise considering toys are sold practically everywhere from grocery stores to hobby shops to hardware stores. Wal-Mart averages the highest toys sales with 19% of the market, followed by Toys R Us with 16.5%. The United States also leads the world in toy development, marketing, and advertising and employs more than 32,000 people in those fields.

World's Largest International Food Franchise

McDonald's

THE WORLD'S LARGEST INTERNATIONAL FOOD FRANCHISES

Number of franchises

McDonald's	Subway	Burger King	KFC	Domino's Pizza
30,078	18,430	11,450	8,624	7,230

There are more than 30,000 McDonald's restaurants in the world, serving customers in 118 different countries. McDonald's serves about 46 million customers each day, about 24 million of whom are in the United States. Some of McDonald's most popular menu items include the Big Mac, the Quarter Pounder, the Egg McMuffin, and Chicken McNuggets. Out of respect for local cultures, restaurants in different countries modify their menus according to religious or cultural traditions. For example, there is a kosher McDonald's in Jerusalem, and the Big Macs in India are made with lamb instead of beef.

U.S. Company with the
Highest-Paid CEOs

Dell Computer

Michael Dell, chief executive officer of Dell Computer, earned more than $201 million in 2002. Dell founded Dell Computer in 1984 with $1,000 in his pocket and a big idea to start a computer business. Headquartered in Austin, Texas, the company specializes in custom-built computer systems and software. Dell has offices throughout the world and employs more than 39,000 people. During Michael Dell's 17 years as CEO the company's sales have jumped from $6 million to $5.4 billion. The 37-year-old Dell is worth $9.8 billion.

AMERICAN COMPANIES WITH THE HIGHEST-PAID CEOs

2002 earnings in millions of US dollars

Dell Computer	JDS Uniphase	Forest Labs	Capital One Financial	Nabors Industries
$201.3 M	$150.8 M	$148.5 M	$142.2 M	$123.7 M

World's Top-Selling Car

Toyota Camry

**THE WORLD'S
TOP-SELLING CARS**

Total sold in 2002

Toyota Camry	Honda Accord	Ford Taurus	Honda Civic	Ford Focus
434,145	398,980	349,742	310,627	286,166

The Toyota Camry was the most popular car in 2002, with sales totaling 434,135 vehicles. The 2002 model featured several upgrades, including a more powerful 157 horsepower engine and an improved emissions system. The Camry has also been rated as one of the safest cars on the road. In addition to front, overhead, and side-impact airbags, the car also features Vehicle Skid Control brakes.

World's
Richest Country

Luxembourg

Luxembourg is a very small country in western Europe. It has a gross domestic product of $42,769 per person. The gross domestic product is calculated by dividing the annual worth of all the goods and services produced in a country by the country's population. Luxembourg's low inflation and low unemployment help to keep the economy solid. The industrial sector makes up a large part of the country's gross domestic product and includes products such as iron and steel, food processing, chemicals, metal products, engineering, tires, glass, and aluminum. The country's financial sector also plays a significant role in the economy, accounting for about 22% of the gross domestic product.

THE WORLD'S RICHEST COUNTRIES

Gross domestic product per capita in US dollars

Luxembourg	USA	Norway	Iceland	Switzerland
$42,769	$31,872	$28,433	$27,835	$27,171

World's
Poorest Country

Sierra Leone

Sierra Leone, a small country on Africa's northwest coast, has a gross domestic product of just $448. Although the country does have solid agricultural, mineral, and fishing resources, the government has not been able to take full advantage of them because of frequent war and social uprising. In the near future, the country hopes to reopen the many mines closed down because of the fighting. Sierra Leone has managed to maintain its diamond mining throughout the wars. The majority of the country makes a living from agriculture and manufacturing. Sierra Leone also receives a large amount of aid from abroad.

THE WORLD'S POOREST COUNTRIES

Gross domestic product per capita in US dollars

Sierra Leone	Tanzania	Burundi	Malawi	Ethiopia
$448	$501	$578	$586	$628

World's Richest Man

Bill Gates

Bill Gates is probably one of the world's most recognizable business-people. He is the co-founder of Microsoft—the most valuable computer software company in the world—and he is worth an incredible $40.7 billion. As Microsoft's largest individual shareholder, Gates became a billionaire on paper when the company went public in 1986. Since then, Gates has been very generous with his fortune. Through his Gates Foundation, he has donated billions of dollars to health research, libraries, and education.

THE WORLD'S RICHEST MEN

Assets in billions of US dollars

Bill Gates, USA	Warren Buffett, USA	Paul Allen, USA	Prince Alwaleed Bin Talal Alsaud, Saudi Arabia	Lawrence Joseph Ellison, USA
$40.7 B	$30.5 B	$20.1 B	$17.7 B	$16.6 B

World's Richest Women

Alice and Helen Walton

With an estimated worth of $16.5 billion each, Helen Walton and her daughter Alice are the richest women in the world. They are two of the heirs to the Walton family fortune, amassed by Helen's husband, entrepreneur Sam Walton. He opened the first Wal-Mart store in 1962 and turned it into one of the most successful businesses in American history. Today, Wal-Mart is the world's largest retailer. The Walton Family Foundation was set up as a way for the Waltons to give back to their country. Schools, church groups, community projects, hospitals, and many other organizations throughout the United States receive donations.

THE WORLD'S RICHEST WOMEN

Assets in billions of US dollars

Alice L. Walton	Helen R. Walton	Lilianne Rettencourt	Barbara Cox Anthony	Anne Cox Chambers
$16.5 B	$16.5 B	$14.5 B	$10.3 B	$10.3 B

Helen Walton

293

World's Youngest Billionaire

Athina Onassis Roussel

Greek shipping tycoon Aristotle Onassis left his granddaughter well provided for. When Athina Onassis Roussel turned 18 years old in 2003, she inherited an estimated $2.7 billion in properties, including an island in the Ionian Sea, companies, shares, artwork, and a private jet. At 21, she will become president of the Athens-based Onassis Foundation and receive another $2 billion. She became the only heir to the Onassis shipping fortune when her mother, Christina, died in 1988. Currently, the estate is being managed by financial advisers. Athina lives in a small village near Lausanne, Switzerland, with her father, Thierry Roussel, and her stepfamily. She speaks fluent English, French, and Swedish, and enjoys playing sports and horseback riding.

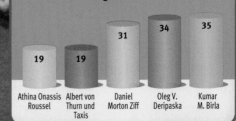

THE WORLD'S YOUNGEST BILLIONAIRES

Age in 2004

Athina Onassis Roussel	Albert von Thurn und Taxis	Daniel Morton Ziff	Oleg V. Deripaska	Kumar M. Birla
19	19	31	34	35

World's All-Time
Richest Person

THE WORLD'S
RICHEST PEOPLE OF ALL TIME

Estimated wealth in current billions of US dollars

$189.0 B				
	$100.0 B	$96.0 B		
			$40.7 B	$30.5 B
John D. Rockefeller	Andrew Carnegie	Cornelius Vanderbilt	Bill Gates	Warren Buffet

John D. Rockefeller's 1913 fortune of $900 million would be worth about $189 billion in current U.S. dollars. Rockefeller made his money from the Standard Oil Company, which he co-founded in 1870. By 1911, he controlled most of the oil production and transportation industries in the United States. Rockefeller was one of the nation's leading philanthropists and was quite generous with his money. In fact, he donated more than $500 million during his lifetime. His son, John Rockefeller, Jr., donated about $2.5 billion of the family fortune to charitable causes.

John D. Rockefeller

Index

Tsunamis, 167
Tuna, 152
Tunnels, 268, 276
Turkey, 173, 266
Turtles, 162
TV, 15–18, 46
Twine, 221
Twins, 240
2001 KX76, 62

U2, 11
UAE, 176, 259
UCLA, 92
Ukraine, 222
United Kingdom, 51, 168, 173, 174, 258, 270, 286
United States, 46–48, 51, 110, 123, 168, 172, 174–176, 191, 257, 260, 262, 266, 270–276, 286
  records, 206–255
Universities, 238
Unser, Al, 98
Unser, Bobby, 98
Uranus, 57, 58, 60, 63, 64
Uruguay, 108, 113
USC, 93
USSR, 123
Utah, 249

Van Gogh, Vincent, 32
Vanderbilt, Cornelius, 295
Vehicles, 35–43
Venezuela, 184
Venus, 56, 59, 65
Vermont, 224, 225, 234, 238, 250
Verrazano-Narrows Bridge, 257
Vesta, 62
Victoria, Lake, 183
Video games, 52
Virginia, 213, 241, 251
Volcano, 165, 204
Voyager of the Seas, 39
Vredefort, 178

Waialeale, Mount, 216
Wal-Mart, 209, 293
Walt Disney Studios, 210
Walton, Alice and Helen, 293
Walton, Sam, 209, 293
Warner Brothers Studio, 210
Washington (state), 204, 217, 219, 233, 252
Washington, D.C., 95, 230, 246

Washington, Mount, 199
Washington Redskins, 71
Water hogs, 138
Water lily, 192
Waterfalls, 184, 227
Watermelon, 169
Wealth, of countries, 290, 291
Wealth, of people, 292–295
Weather, 199–204
Web sites, 49, 50
Weeds, 194
Wenchuan, China, 265
Wessig, Gerd, 111
West Edmonton Mall, 263
West, Jerry, 88
West Virginia, 253
West Wing, The (TV show), 18
Whale shark, 151
Whales, 136, 139
Wheat, 189
Williams, Billy, 75
Williams, Robbie, 6
Willis, Bruce, 21
Wills-Moody, Helen, 105
Wind, 199
Wingspan, 141, 148
Winston Cup, 99
Wisconsin, 227, 254
Witt, Katarina, 101, 121
WNBA, 90, 91
Wockel, Barbel Eckert, 117
Wolf 359, 61
Women, 293
  art, 33
  movies, 20
  music, 13
  sports, 90, 91, 93, 101, 103, 105, 107, 110, 115, 117, 119, 121
  television, 16
Women's National Basketball Association, 90, 91
World Cup, 108, 109
World Series, 85
World Wide Web, 48, 49, 51
Wrangell-St. Elias, 207
Wrigley Field, 226
Wyoming, 221, 231, 255

Yachts, 37
Yagudin, Alexei, 120
Yahoo!, 50
Yangtze River, 185
Yankee Stadium, 226
Yankees, 85, 211
Yarborough, Cale, 99

Yastrzanski, Carl, 87
Yegorov, Boris B., 55
Yellow River, 163
Yellowstone National Park, 255
Yenisei-Angara River, 185
Yosemite, 184, 255, 269
Yukong, 259

Zany Brainy, 235

wild wacky AND amazing FACTS

Toys and Games • Sports
Entertainment
Structures
Food • Animals

Speaking of Spuds

When he was introduced in 1952, Mr. Potato Head contained only parts—such as eyes, ears, noses, and mouths—and parents had to supply children with real potatoes. Eight years later, he got his plastic body. Quickly gaining popularity, Mr. Potato Head became the official "spokespud" for the American Cancer Society's annual "Great American Smokeout" in 1987. Ten years later, Burger King hired him to be the spokespud for the introduction of their new french fries.

A Model of Success

Originally, Play-Doh® Brand Modeling Compound was developed in 1956 as a wallpaper cleaning product. Today, approximately 2.5 million cans of Play-Doh are manufactured each week, with retail sales topping approximately $150 million worldwide. Play-Doh is sold in 21 countries around the world.

Stretching Sales

Around 250 million Slinkys have been sold since 1952. Each regular-size metal Slinky contains 80 feet (24.4 m) of coiled wire. More than 3 million miles (4.8 million km) of wire—or 50,000 tons (45,350 t)—have been used in the Slinky's 51 years of production.

A Hot Commodity

More than 1.5 billion Hot Wheels® have been produced since 1968—more vehicles than have been built by Detroit's three largest car manufacturers combined. The number of these tiny toy vehicles sold over the past 30 years is equivalent to about two every second. More than 1,000 different Hot Wheels models have been created, and the Corvette is the most popular.

Block Party

About 189 billion LEGO® pieces have been produced since their invention in 1949. Some 300 million children and adults all over the world have played with these LEGO bricks. Every year, children spend almost 5 billion hours playing with LEGOs. And all of this playtime can be put to good use—there are 102,981,500 different ways to combined six 8-stud LEGO bricks of the same color.

What's in a Name?

There are only two towns in the country that have been named after professional football players—Jim Thorpe, Pennsylvania, and Joe, Montana. Thorpe played football for the Canton Bulldogs from 1920 to 1928. Thorpe also played professional baseball and competed in the 1912 Olympics, leading the Associated Press to declare him "Athlete of the Half Century" in 1950. Montana was a record-setting quarterback for the San Francisco 49ers and the Kansas City Chiefs, and played from 1979 to 1994.

Wild Thing!

Nolan Ryan has thrown the most wild pitches in Major League Baseball with 277. And because of the strength with which he threw the ball, some major league hitters, including Reggie Jackson, were a little nervous to face him at the plate for fear of injury! Nicknamed The Ryan Express, the pitching powerhouse spent his 27-year career with the Mets, Astros, Angels, and Rangers. Ryan retired from baseball in 1993 after striking out 5,714 batters and winning 324 games.

During his career, Kareem Abdul-Jabbar had 4,657 fouls in his 1,560 games—the most of any NBA player. He once missed 20 games because he broke his hand in a fight with another player. Standing more than 7 feet (2.1 m) tall, Abdul-Jabbar also had an intimidating "sky hook." This trademark jump helped him score an amazing 38,387 career points.

Does Someone Need a Timeout?

Hey, Give Those Back!

Ricky Henderson has gotten caught stealing 335 bases during his career, the most of any major league player. He has successfully stolen 1,403 bases, giving him an 81% success rate. Henderson began his major league career in 1979 with the Oakland Athletics. Since then, he has played for the Yankees, Blue Jays, Padres, Angels, Mets, Mariners, and Red Sox.

That's Going to Leave a Mark

Quarterback David Carr of the Houston Texans got sacked an unbelievable 76 times in only 16 games during 2002—the team's first season in the NFL. That averages out to almost 5 sacks each game. Carr did manage to pick up 2,592 yards and complete 9 touchdowns while dodging the competition. He ended the season with 4 wins and a quarterback rating of 62.8.

Animation Sensation

There are 36 unique locations in *Shrek*—more than any other computer-animated film. Computer animation production took more than four and a half years to complete, but critics felt it was worth the wait. This film was the first winner for the inaugural Best Animated Feature Film category of the Academy Awards® 2002.

X-cellent Costume

For Hugh Jackman's Wolverine character in *X-Men*, 10 costumes were built out of thick leather and PVC. All of them were destroyed to some extent during filming. There were 3 types of Wolverine claw—plastic, wood, and steel. More than 700 individual claw blades were used by Jackman and his 4 stunt doubles.

Mummy Mishaps

Was there really a curse of the mummy? Brendan Fraser, who played Rick O'Connell, passed out while filming a scene for *The Mummy* because the noose around his neck was too tight. A few years later, on the set of the sequel, Fraser tore a spinal disk, cracked a rib, and injured his knees during production. And the Scorpion King, played by Dwayne Johnson (also known as The Rock), suffered from food poisoning and sunstroke.

Dog-Gone Beautiful

Apparently everyone in Hollywood needs to keep up their looks. For *Men in Black II*, the original pug from the first movie was used again to play Frank. But, since the pug was now 7 years old, makeup artists had to hide the gray fur around his nose and in his coat.

Potter's Word Puzzles

J. K. Rowling likes to play with words. The Hogwarts motto, "draco dormiens nunquam titillandus" means "never tickle a sleeping dragon" in Latin. The inscription around the Mirror of Erised says, "Erised stra ehru oyt ube cafru oyt on wohsi." Reading the inscription backward, it says, "I show not your face but your heart's desire."

Malcolm's Mysteries

Malcolm in the Middle—FOX's hit comedy about a dysfunctional family with 3 sons—has some mysteries. For instance, no one knows where this fictional family actually lives or what their last name is. And while mom Lois works in the drug store, her husband Hal's job has never been disclosed.

Matrix Money Madness

The Matrix Reloaded was quite a pricey film to produce. One 17-minute battle scene alone cost more than $40 million. The movie's special effects cost $100 million. But at least one thing came for free—GM donated 300 cars for use in the production of the movie. Unfortunately, all of them were wrecked by the end!

Idol Insanity

In Fall 2002, more than 70,000 contestants auditioned for the second season of FOX's *American Idol*. The final two contestants were Ruben Studdard and Clay Aiken. Almost 26 million viewers tuned in to the finale on May 21, 2003, making it the third-highest reality show audience in history. After a record 24 million votes were cast, Studdard was crowned the winner.

Dynamite Dino Droppings

In *Jurassic Park III*, the *Spinosaurus* was the largest animatronic ever built. It weighed 12 tons (10.8 t) and was operated by hydraulics. This allowed it to work while completely submerged in water. During production, the effects crew used 250 gallons (1.1 billion l) of oatmeal to simulate Spinosaur droppings.

Take This to Heart

Each year, Necco produces 8 billion Sweethearts® Conversation Hearts around Valentine's Day. The annual production of these sweet treats would stretch from New York to Los Angeles and back again. In 2003, Necco designed their new heart sayings around the importance of literacy, including the phrases, "WHIZ KID," "LET'S READ," "WISE UP," and "WRITE ME."

Sweethearts
Necco®
NET WT
1 1/8 OZ
32g

Lions and Tigers and Bears, Oh My

Each hour, Nabisco produces 15,000 cartons of animal crackers containing 300,000 cookies. Each year, some 8,000 miles (12,880 km) of string are used as handles on the boxes. There have been 54 different animals produced since 1902, but only 4 have survived all 101 years—lions, tigers, bears, and elephants.

BARNUM'S ANIMALS
★ CRACKERS ★
NABISCO
LION
GORILLA
POLAR BEAR
ELEPHANT
NET WT
2½ OZ
(60g)
GOOD SOURCE OF
CALCIUM

Marshmallow Madness

Food manufacturer Just Born can produce a marshmallow Peep in just 6 minutes, and machines can paint on 3,800 Peep eyes per minute. Yellow Peeps are the best-sellers, followed by pink, lavender, blue, and white. Recently, Just Born introduced red, white, and blue Patriotic Peeps. Some people do odd things with their Peeps, such as freeze them, roast them, microwave them, and use them as pizza toppings.

A Sticky Situation

The average American child will eat 1,500 peanut-butter sandwiches before he or she graduates from high school. Americans eat an average of 3 pounds (1.4 kg) of the sticky stuff each year, totaling about 840 million pounds (381 million kg)— enough to cover the floor of the Grand Canyon! That's also enough peanut butter to make 12 billion PB&J sandwiches.

It Can Sure Take A Lickin'

How many licks does it take to get to the center of a Tootsie Pop? Well, some Purdue University students built a licking machine to find out. The machine averaged 364 licks, but a group of volunteers averaged 252 licks. Many factors can influence the outcome, including saliva produced and mouth size. So, the world may truly never know.

Luckily They Didn't Charge By the Pound

Ohio's Great American Ball Park—home of the Cincinnati Reds—is made of 10,100 tons (9,161 t) of structural steel. That is the equivalent of 9.8 billion paper clips, or enough to make a paper clip chain that would circle the globe nearly eight times. The Model 999 crane, used to install most of the structural steel at the Great American Ball Park, has enough lifting power to simultaneously hoist 192 Volkswagen Beetles.

A Chilly Check-In

The Ice Hotel in Quebec, Canada, is a working hotel that is sculpted completely of ice. Covering a total surface of 30,000 square feet (2,787 sq m), the Ice Hotel uses 350 tons (317 t) of ice each season to completely rebuild this architectural marvel. The hotel's 4-foot- (1.2-m) thick walls help to maintain a constant temperature of about 28° Fahrenheit (-2.2° C). The hotel has many rooms, a cinema, a chapel, functional fireplaces, and hot tubs.

Can You Dig It?

The city of Boston, Massachusetts, has spent $10 billion to create the Central Artery/Tunnel—affectionately nicknamed The Big Dig. When completed in 2004, the tunnel will be eight lanes wide and 3.5 miles (5.6 km) long. The project has moved 15 million cubic yards of dirt—enough to fill a football stadium 15 times. It took 541,000 truck-loads to move all of this dirt!

Raising the Roof

The Georgia Dome is the largest cable-supported dome stadium in the world and can seat up to 80,000 people. The Georgia Dome also has the largest cable-supported fabric roof in the world. Although the 395,000-square-foot (37,000-sq-m) roof weighs only 68 pounds (31 kg), it can support the weight of a dump truck.

What an Appetite!

A bird will eat half of its weight in food each day. If an 8-year-old child were to do the same, he or she would polish off about 30 pounds (13.6 kg) of food—or about 150 hamburgers. So much for eating like a bird!

Freezing Frogs

Woodland frogs are the only animals that are able to survive after they have been frozen. These frogs live north of the Arctic circle and survive for weeks in a frozen state. Glucose in their blood acts as a kind of antifreeze. This protects their vital organs from damage while the rest of the body is frozen solid.

Prickly Poison

One hedgehog may have as many as 8,000 spines. To make themselves even more unappealing to predators, hedgehogs will chew on certain poisonous leaves to which they are immune. They will then spit out the poisonous saliva and coat their prickly spines with it.